Baba À Louis Bakery Bread Book

BABA À LOUIS BAKERY BREAD BOOK

The Secret Book of the Bread

by John McLure

Baba À Louis Bakery, Proctorsville, Vermont

First published in the USA by
Baba À Louis Bakery,
Box 41, Chester, Vermont 05143

Development, design, and production by
The Laughing Bear Associates,
2 Downing Street, Montpelier, Vermont 05602

Distributed by
Chelsea Green Publishing Company,
PO Box 130, Post Mills, Vermont 05058

ISBN 0-9636892-0-7

Library of Congress Catalog
Card Number: 93-78237

Dedication

This book is dedicated to Anita Deloch and Nancy Lockerby, without whom the bread or this book would not be delivered.

This dedication is in honor of them for giving life and energy to baking beyond the call of duty and beyond my capacity to keep the bakery going.

Acknowledgments

I would like to thank Mary and Allon Schoener for encouraging me to start on the first steps of this quest. I thank Alain Kleinberger and Veronique Gallet, without whom I would never have found the historical background for this book.

I would like to thank Alessandro Zezza, Tonya Sammartino, Mary McCallum, and Ellen Foscue Johnson for their efforts to capture bread making on film.

I would like to thank Eric Fournet for his vital information; Linda Iskander for her vision and literary suggestions; Peter Farrar for his intuition and simplicity; Mary Ormrod for her testing and cooperation; Christopher Fitz and Shelley Pike for contributing their youthful enthusiasm and for their prediction that a book such as this might someday be written; Jerry Sojouner for his partnership and support; Ugo Quazzo for his innovative contributions; Hugh Taft for his literary contributions; Earl Shangraw for keeping our machinery alive; and Arthur and Tibby Bratton, Karl Pfister, and J. R. Leonard for their encouraging gifts.

I give many thanks to all the customers of the Baba À Louis Bakeries.

I would like to thank Tom Duncan for having been co-creator of recipes and for having been at the bakery assuming my responsibilities so that I had the time for this book.

I would most of all like to thank Ruth Zezza who untangled my writing. I also give great thanks to Jean-Carlo McLure for sharing his father's time and attention with this project.

TABLE OF CONTENTS

Be gentle
When you touch Bread
Let it not lie
Uncared for...unwanted
So often
Bread is taken for granted
There is so much beauty
In Bread
Beauty of sun and soil
Beauty of patient toil
Winds and rain have caressed it
Christ so often blessed it
Be gentle when you touch Bread

Old Scottish Verse

The Secret Book of the Bread

12

The Making of Bread

The making of bread is elemental—calling for earth, air, fire, and water in the right proportion and in nature's time. In the meeting of earth, as present in broken grain, and spirit, as expressed through the hands of the baker, bread becomes the balancing point of life for the person with eyes to see.

Sensual and spiritual, symbol of both simplicity and transcendent mystery, bread rewards the baker in each step of its creation but achieves its true purpose only when broken and shared. This vehicle of life then becomes, somehow, us, and the cycle continues.

This book is presented with the hope the reader will take the time to enjoy the making of bread and the sharing of it with many others in happiness and health.

Peter Farrar
Andover, Vermont

Left: 1887 painting by the French artist Madame Demont Breton.

Esurij multa Cereris
me fruge cibastis

14

The Decline of Bread

With malice toward none; with charity for all.
Abraham Lincoln

People's tastes vary and tastes are emotionally bound to an individual's culture. As old cultures are being overrun, so too the function of bread has altered to fit modern living. Bread has gone from being a main staple to a fast food envelope.

In France, the consumption of bread is declining. According to the *Guide de L'Amateur de Pain*, in 1980 the consumption was about half what it was in 1950 and about one-fifth as much as in the eighteenth and nineteenth centuries.

The production of bread has been taken on by the mercenary enterprises of our time. The quality of the bread has been sacrificed for speed, money, and shelf life. The flour is stripped of its cumbersome bran and germ coatings; then vitamins, additives, and preservatives are sprayed back on. It is very difficult to buy a flour that has not been "enriched."

This sped-up bread production has taken hold in the United States and other Anglo-Saxon countries. It is especially prevalent in England where as much as 70 percent of the bread is produced in this manner, according to *La Biochemie du Pain*. Around-the-clock productions, where they use this "no-time dough," have eliminated any rising time. This process of forcing dough down conduit pipes and making chemical alterations to it has adapted bread to the impatience of an industrialized world.

The decline of bread may have reached bottom. Without blaming anyone, the task now is to find ingredients that have not been compromised by mass production and to create ways of making bread as simple and as wholesome as possible.

"Going back to the old ways" is a confusing slogan. It is my notion that good wholesome bread can adapt to changes despite the self-destructive path of technology. This book has something for all tastes and can help reverse the decline of bread.

John McLure

Left: Early French engraving representing bread merchants and the attributes of the baker.

Bread and Thoughts

Saint Honoré

Saint Honoré, the Patron Saint of Bakers, is celebrated on 16 May. He originated in the region of Abbeville and was head of the diocese of Amiens in the sixth century.

During a long drought in 1060, a procession was given in honor of Saint Honoré in Amiens, imploring him to help. Before the ceremony was finished, it started pouring and many miraculous healings were reported to have occurred. The Saint Honoré Cult was thus born and started spreading throughout France.

In 1204, his renown reached Paris. Thus a couple of the noble Picards erected, on the right bank of the Seine, a beautiful gothic church which they dedicated to him. (Having become part of the church collegiate system, it was destroyed in the 1790 revolution.)

The bakers, who worked the ovens of the Louvre situated right across the way, established their brotherhood or guild in this church and naturally consecrated it to the saint. From that time on, Saint Honoré was represented with the attributes of the baking profession.

Other information indicates that the bakers chose him as a patron in the memory of a miracle where some divine hand presented him with bread (eucharist) while he was celebrating a mass.

The previous patrons of the bakers' guild of Paris were Pierre aux Lien and Saint Lazare.

Left: St. Honoré, the Patron Saint of Bakers.

The Cake

We had our flour in a trash can underneath our calendar. We used the calendar to write down any unusual orders we might have. At the time there were very few of those, so each one was an exciting proposition.

A brave man came to the bakery and ordered a cake for his wife. We will not include his name here; if he has forgotten about the affair, we would like that to remain the status quo. Both he and his wife were around the age of retirement. He wanted to make very sure that we would remember to make this cake for his wife, so he ordered this cake three or four weeks in advance. That sounded like a good idea to us and he seemed reassured to know that we were writing it down. In the meantime, the calendar was swept off the wall along with the thumb tack which held it on the wall. Both the calendar and the tack went into the trash can into the flour . . . all this right in front of us.

We plunged in after the two fallen items and found the tack in the last batch of flour that was sifted. In all the excitement we decided that was no place for a calendar. We folded it up and put it somewhere to be forgotten until one day this brave and trusting man came in for his cake. He asked for his cake the way someone who is sure of something does—with a calm and careless attitude, slightly arrogant. Of course the cake had long since been forgotten, never mind made, so the questioned baker came into the back room and we had a conference.

It was decided that one of us had to go out there and tell him. He was mad, expressed himself well, and left in a huff. We conferred again after he left and decided that the cake indeed could be made with a great deal of effort, so we called him. When he answered the phone, he was pleasant. When he was told that the cake could be made for him, he remained pleasant but said that it was okay he wouldn't have it. We took this experience as a lesson. Orders need to be made the day before and sometimes there is no way to repair the damage— some people would rather be mad.

Right: "La Boulangère."
This statue by Contan formerly stood at the foot of La Tour St. Jacques.

Health

After two years of running the bakery, I wondered about the condition of my health. I spent a year without leaving town and lived almost exclusively at the bakery. I ate irregularly, poorly, and often. The most common snack I remember was bread and cheese; I can't remember eating any vegetables. I put on weight during this time.

One day, as I jumped off a back shed (only two feet off the ground), my legs buckled. I put my arms out to catch myself. My arms slowly gave way until my nose was in the garden dirt. Picking myself up out of the rhubarb patch, I realized that parts of my body were becoming atrophied.

The next time my general condition attracted my attention was during winter of that year. I felt a need for exercise so I thought I should go to the high school and play basketball. I was familiar with this sport and the activity would presumably help me get fit. As I was warming up, it felt as though I had no flesh on the bottoms of my feet. It was as if the basketball court were beating against the bones of my feet. I didn't let that bother me as I joined the others on the court.

For the most part, the players were all 30 to 40 years of age, and we were all there for the same reason, apparently. As the game started, the group of players ran down one side of the court. As we came back to the other side, I felt my ankle sprain.

No one was near me, I had not touched the ball, and the game had been going for only eight seconds. I crawled to the side lines as one of the players passed by and said: "That was quick."

On top of this, I became ill that night. I had not allowed myself to become sick for two years, but now congestion settled in. I went to bed and when I woke up early to work in the bakery, the congestion filled my head. I felt as if cotton were stuffed in my ears and up my sinuses, and worst of all, my sprained ankle was sore.

The fun started. I had to roll the bread, put it in canvases, and then on trays. Then it had to be taken to the proof box (a box with a door especially designed for the rising of dough). It was only a short distance for someone on two legs, but because I had only one functioning leg, the routine changed dramatically. I had to hold the tray on one hand just like a waiter and hop the length of the bakery to get to the proof box holding myself whenever I could with the other hand and then hop back to the dough box empty-handed. The soreness of the bottom of my one good foot was acute. It was one of the longest nights I can remember. I had a chair nearby and I spent time in the chair in between batches. I concluded that my health would have to improve.

Chain Cake

I received a chain cake. The instructions indicated that I must pass on part of the soured batter or else risk dire consequences. However, if I did pass on the batter, I would release myself from risk and indebt the next fortunates: to pass it on or take the consequences.

By the time I got around to reading the note, the due date was nearly up. My solution was to shape the batter on a sheet pan into an ankh (the ancient Egyptian symbol for eternal life). I baked it and fed it to our pet pig.

"We make ourselves to be exactly what we are; and we are, at the same time, our brothers' keeper because each one of us, each one of us, is responsible for an aeonic chain of causation. . . . We cannot think or speak or act without affecting other beings, to their weal or to their woe." (*Gift of the Lotus* compiled by Virginia Hanson.)

Overtime

I am in the process of rolling rolls. There is more bread to roll than there is time to roll it. The proof boxes (where the dough rises) are half full of rolls. The ovens are on and bread needs to go into the oven. I am busy rolling rolls and more rolls. I am rolling rolls for hours. Then I look for my knife. It is lost. I can't find it. I run back and forth. It is the only knife I have. I finally find the knife. I cut more dough and roll some more. I need to do much more before I can start baking. Finally one of the proof boxes is full so I go to the second or third . . . I don't remember. I roll some more rolls. I am carrying a tray of rolls to place them into the next proof box. I make an attempt to move one of the boxes. They seem extremely tall.

All of a sudden the proof box that is full begins to lean toward me. I lunge to catch it and the next proof box begins to tip sideways. I am desperately holding them both. They are swaying like trees in a wind storm and a disagreeable sound rings at my side.

I awake and shut off my alarm clock. I get up and look out the window at a cool peaceful night. It is 1 or 2 AM. Time to go downstairs underneath our apartment and start the day at Baba À Louis Bakery. Everything is right where it should be. I grab my knife, cut some dough, and start rolling rolls.

21

When you blow your breath on a cold window pane, the frost that appears is part of you just as the plants we "feed" with our radiations are part of us. We are, in fact, all part of one thing, all different materializations of the one life.

The Findhorn Garden
by the Findhorn Community

Baking Processes

Measuring

To avoid needless disappointment, it is important to weigh the flour and to get accurate cup measurements of liquids because everyone has varying baking methods and conditions can never be the same. If the flour is weighed exactly and the liquid measured to perfection, you will get a consistent start. There are, however, some recipes where flour is listed only in cups because the weight of the flour is not vital.

In the Hall of Receipts (page 119), the measurements are for large batches. The flour must be weighed out or you will not be able to adjust with the changing of seasons. In the winter season when the atmosphere is drier, more water is required. In the summer when the atmosphere is humid, less water is required. When the doors and windows are closed from autumn throughout winter, adjustments and moisture are constant.

At home it may be possible to convert from accurately weighed flour to cup measured, but learn to judge the doughs by their appearances first. The accuracy of the measurements stated in the recipes, as well as the appropriate proportions for large or small recipes, is vital for all the recipes and crucial for the naturally leavened and the soured yeast breads.

About Yeast

First we will introduce instant yeast, which is very small pellets of yeast manufactured by combining tiny yeast particles with small amounts of alkalized vegetable fats, potato starch, and soy oil. It does not require dissolving in water and can be thrown in directly with the dry ingredients. The mixing will take care of the rest. This instant yeast is usually vacuum-packed in aluminum packs with no preservatives. Once the seal on these packs is broken, the yeast does not last as long as dry pellet yeast.

Instant yeast is relatively new although it is widely used in the baking industry. It is not available in supermarkets, but some health food stores and specialty cooking catalogues sell it. The easiest way to acquire instant yeast is to buy it from commercial bakers in a 1-pound pack. It also comes in 5- or 6-ounce packs or an 11-gram pack (1 tablespoon).

The advantage in using instant yeast is that hot water can be thrown into the mixture with little concern about killing the yeast. By the time the cold bowl and the cool ingredients have counteracted the heat of the water, the instant yeast has a good warm start. In this book, the yeast is listed in quantities for instant yeast.

As for the dry yeast, it needs to be at least softened with water and usually diluted and poured in with some liquid which must not be hot. This requires more steps and you should be very vigilant about subtracting the water used to dissolve the yeast from the overall water required for the recipe.

Compressed yeast can also be used as an instant yeast especially with a commercial mixer. Crumble it into the dry ingredients and mix it in thoroughly. For the soured yeast breads that have firm dough and a long rising time, this is excellent. French bakers, until the arrival of instant yeast, always used and still use compressed yeast. For more delicate recipes, compressed yeast should be softened by diluting it in water. Compressed yeast is often a by-product of the beer industry.

Yeast Conversion Table

All the recipes in this book use instant yeast. Below are guidelines for converting measurements if you wish to use other kinds of yeast.

Instant Yeast		Compressed Yeast
1 tsp.	→	3 tsp.
1 Tb.	→	3 Tb.
1 oz.	→	3 oz.

Instant Yeast		Dry Yeast
¾ tsp.	→	1 tsp.
¾ Tb.	→	1 Tb.
¾ oz.	→	1 oz.

The purpose of life, then, is not
the gratifying of appetites nor of
any selfish desires, but it is that
the entity, the soul, may make
the earth where the entity finds
its consciousness, a better place
in which to live.

Edgar Cayce

Soured Yeast Breads

Even if you don't want to make French bread, reading through the Basic French Bread recipe is a prerequisite to making the other soured yeast breads. Essential to these breads is the 12-hour rise which contributes to their particular flavor and texture.

By reading this section in the order it is presented, you will be able to see the evolution of the recipes.

Basic French Bread

(makes two 1½-pound loaves)

Our French bread recipe came about gradually and developed from mishaps, as well as from my memory of what French bread is like. When I went back to France to try standard French bread, I realized that something was different. This bread kept its moisture, was more dense, and had the tanginess of a real sour bread. It was less delicate in appearance. When baked well in a hot oven, it developed a dark crust that sometimes crackled and shined. It had relatively large holes in its flesh. (A bread is made up of a crust and the insides. For our purpose, the insides will be referred to as the flesh.) It kept well and by the next day was very tasty with its particular odor and crispness still present instead of having a styrofoam look. It froze well. It came back to life with ease. It was praised. It was liked. My apprenticeship was spent finding out what conditions were most favorable for making this French bread.

The process I learned and have outlined in this Basic French Bread recipe is the foundation of all the soured yeast recipes which follow it. Even if you don't want to make French bread, reading through this recipe will give you information that will help you in making all the other breads.

This recipe is also the starting point of some of the other breads of the bakery. Mixing Basic French Bread dough into other recipes creates a dough which holds its shape better than if started with all dry ingredients and yields a bread with a more buoyant texture. Excess Basic French Bread dough can be frozen and will later make an excellent pizza dough or can be mixed into Sourdough Rye, Lenten, and other soured yeast breads.

The only requirement for making this bread is an oven which will heat up to 475°F (245°C) and stay there for 20 minutes. It is more important to have a scale than a mixer. The lack of a scale should not be used as an excuse for not making this bread. Anybody can make Basic French Bread.

◆

☞ Please read through all procedures of this recipe before attempting the mixture.

Atmospheric Conditions

Using warm water for the yeast, the best results are attained at steady temperatures between 61–75°F (16°–23°C). A temperature of around 68°F (20°C) accompanied by a rainy or humid day provides ideal conditions for this bread.

When the room temperature is cooler, 40–60°F (5–14°C), you may increase the water by 1 tablespoon. The water can be hot, 140°F (60°C). You must separate the yeast from the rest of the recipe. The hot water will cool as it is mixed with colder flour and a cold bowl. Add the instant yeast or dissolved yeast and mix as stated before. In 12 hours everything will be cooled off. Under these colder conditions, the dough may need to rise longer than 12 hours.

For temperatures over 75°F (24°C), you can compensate by taking 1 tablespoon of water at a time away from the basic recipe. Remember that the dough has got to be tough. Increasing the salt (1 teaspoon for the recipe) and using cold tap water are methods to use when the temperature reaches around 90°F (32°C).

About Flour

Flours vary considerably even when made from the same sort of wheat. The biggest problem we have noticed is the moisture absorption of different flours. All-purpose flour takes as much as 20 percent more moisture to get the same result as bread flours having the same brand name. With an all-purpose flour (most stores carry all-purpose flour), you may have to increase the water to 2¼ cups for this French bread as well as all the sourdough types. Note that it is only after the 12-hour rise that one should be concerned about a too dry or tough dough. I was once given a recipe that said: "Add as much water as is needed." The whole point is to know the quantities of moisture needed. What feels good at mixing time doesn't always mean it will be fine for baking 12 hours later.

These sour breads tend to start off being relatively tough. Do not add water and after 12 hours they will be more malleable. If the dough should happen to be very tough after the 12-hour rise, then this is the time to add a small amount of water to the dough: 1 tablespoon of water at a time is mixed in well until the dough looks lively but firm.

All-purpose flours have 11.5 percent gluten protein instead of about 12.5 percent in bakers' bread flours. Because of the lengthy rising times required for this recipe, this gluten difference can be minimized.

About Mixing

Generally the more thoroughly the dough is mixed the less time it takes for the dough to rise. During hot weather, 80°F(26°C) and up, the rising process can be slowed down by undermixing the dough. When the dough is undermixed, it appears lumpy and irregular. During cooler or cold weather, 79°F (25°C) and below, mix the dough long enough for it to acquire a smooth and velvety look. The 12-hour rise helps to even out the differences in the mixing. Mixing the dough for a long time incorporates air into the bread. This activates the yeast, lightens the texture of the bread, and bleaches out the color of the flesh.

In France, standard equipment is a high-speed mixer. They beat their dough and the result is a whiteness of the flesh of the bread. This is the same principle as whipping egg whites for a meringue. However, the mixer is not a crucial tool to make this bread dough; your hands are all you need for mixing this bread recipe.

A customer who once worked at a commercial bakery told me that where he worked ice-cold water was mixed with the flour because the mixing was done with such speed and intensity that the dough would otherwise overheat during mixing.

Mixing and kneading are not the same thing. With mechanical mixers, mixing and kneading happen simultaneously. Without a mixer, the dough is mixed with a wooden spoon or by hand until it is unable to be stirred; then the dough is kneaded with both hands until it hangs together and is relatively smooth.

About Ovens

Any kind of home oven will bake bread. You don't need to buy a special oven. The ovens which get publicity for making bread have very little importance in making wonderful bread. The bigger the oven the more you can make, but that does not affect the quality.

Tools

☞ Essentials:

◆ *a 1-cup measure*
◆ *a 1-Tb. measure*
◆ *a 1-tsp. measure*
◆ *a bowl with an 8-cup capacity and cover (or plastic bag)*
◆ *a cornmealed sheet pan*
◆ *a sharp knife*
◆ *hot mitts*
◆ *a hot oven (wood, gas, or electric)*

☞ Other beneficial tools:

◆ *a scale*
◆ *a mixer*
◆ *a roasting pan to cover the sheet pan for the second rise*
◆ *a cooling rack*

Measuring

Accuracy in weights and measures is vital to successful French bread. You should always weigh the flour, but the water measure or weight is even more important. A tablespoon one way or the other will make a difference. Salt and yeast require accurate spoon measures.

Basic Timing

The emphasis of this recipe is on the correct proportions of the ingredients and on the conditions that favor the dough's long rising time.

1. Mixing and kneading
2. 12-hour rise
3. Shaping
4. 3-hour rise
5. Baking at 475°F (245°C) for about 20 minutes

The Procedure

☞ Knead together:

- *2 lb. unbleached white flour (6½ cups unsifted)*
- *1 tsp. instant yeast (page 24) (1½ tsp. dry yeast dissolved in water below)*
- *3½ tsp. sea salt*
- *2 cups + 2 Tb. water, anywhere from body temperature to 120°F (48°C)*

The dough is tough. Do not be tempted to add water except as described in About Flour (page 30). Twelve hours later you will find a dough with a shiny surface; sinkholes or craters the size of coins made by fallen bubbles; and, when stretched out, a stringy spiderweb look (photo, page 34). This signifies a fine sour-tasting bread.

When you mix the dough at 9 o'clock at night, you can start shaping the loaves at about 9:00 the next morning or whenever the dough looks ready (photo, page 35). The French bread could be out in time for lunch. In warmer weather of 80–90°F, the process is sped up to a 9-hour first rising and a 1- to 2-hour second rising.

35

After the 12-hour rise, knock down the dough and mold it into whatever shape desired. This recipe will make two 1½-pound loaves or, for French bread, two 24-inch long loaves. Most home ovens take trays of 12 × 18 inches. Therefore three 1-pound loaves of about 18-inches long are possible. Twelve 4-ounce rolls may be placed on a similar tray that has been sprinkled with cornmeal. We use whole or yellow cornmeal to line our sheet pans for all our sour-type breads that are not put in bread pans.

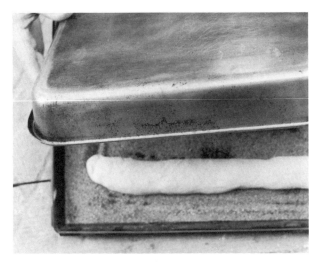

 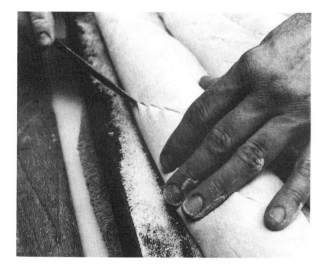

Place your assortment of French breads to rise a second time until double in diameter. This should be as long as 3 hours. Ideal rising conditions are a moist and warm environment. If you cover the tray of rising French with a roasting pan that is moist on the inside, you will get a shiny, moist, and almost tacky surface on the bread dough. If your bread does not have this moist surface, do not be concerned. It will be less pretty, but no less tasty.

With a sharp knife or a razor blade, make some diagonal slices into the loaves in order to release pressure and avoid bulging out the sides.

This bread cooks at 475°F (245°C). For small ovens it is advisable to preheat to 500°F (260°C); lower to about 450°F (230°C) when placing the bread in the oven.

 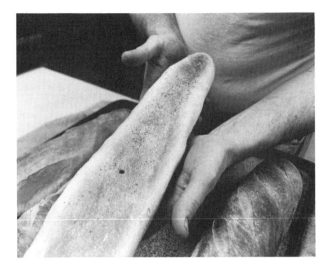

If you want to add steam to the process of cooking the French bread, this is the time to do so. Steam is used to improve the appearance and texture of the loaf. The surface, as a result, will be more resilient and crackly. A couple of tablespoons of water thrown onto a hot surface inside of the oven will create steam which will adhere to the moist tacky surface of the French bread. If the bread has developed a dry and crusty surface before being placed in the oven, the steam will have little effect.

In commercial ovens, the bread should cook in 20 minutes, but with smaller ovens one should check at 15 minutes. Before baking is completed, rotate the bread around on the tray to assure even cooking. It is very difficult to give a precise baking time. The different shapes and volumes of bread along with variations in ovens will require different cooking times. The French bread is done when it has a light brown crispy bottom.

Rye Mix

When we first ordered rye flour for our rye bread, the flour was an unsifted blend of coarse pieces of rye and of fine rye flour. Unbeknownst to us at the time, this mixture of flours is known as unbolted rye flour.

This coarse rye flour has the advantage of incorporating more actual rye and more rye flavor with the grainy consistency primitive breads had in the Old World.

The fine ground rye flour has the disadvantage of weighing the bread down and making the texture more gummy for equal amounts of rye flour. The hearty texture is lost to a heavier, brick-like block of bread.

We would not have known that there is a range of grind to choose from if the rye flour had come all finely ground. The distributor explained that the mill had had problems but that from then on we would have only finely ground rye flour.

Maur's Rye

It was a stroke of luck for us that the flour mill had not been functioning properly. Our rye breads would never have had their character and may have been disbanded altogether had we not had "faulty" flour to start off with.

Our only recourse was to create our own unbolted rye. Rye flakes (available in most health-food stores) along with chopped rye mixed with fine rye flour in the proportions stated below was the solution. This is a recipe for an unbolted rye flour which we use in all our rye breads.

◆

☞ Mix one part fine rye flour with one part cracked rye berries (rye berries chopped into 2 or 3 chunks) and/or rye flakes. Measure by weight not by volume as the chopped rye contains more air than the rye flour. The same chopped rye can be obtained by grinding rye berries in a home meat grinder, wheat grinder, or blender and then adding the rye flour.

- *1 lb. Rye Mix (page 40) (2 ¾ cups)*
- *1 lb. whole wheat flour (3 cups)*
- *¾ lb. unbleached white flour (2½ cups)*
- *1½ tsp. sea salt*
- *1½ tsp. caraway seeds*
- *1½ tsp. seaweed (powdered or shredded)*
- *1 tsp. instant yeast (page 24)*
- *3½ cups water, anywhere from body temperature to120°F (48°C)*

Incorporate ¾ pounds of the Basic French Bread dough (page 35), soured or not, into the above and allow to rise for 12 hours at room temperature (62°–65°F, 18°C). Weigh out 3 loaves and let them rise in loaf pans and bake for 40 minutes at 350°F (175°C).

Sourdough Rye

There are two ways to go about making this bread. You can use the straight recipe here to make a richer-in-rye sourdough rye, or you can mix in a portion of the Basic French Bread recipe to make a lighter rye bread.

- *12 oz. Rye Mix (page 40) (2 cups + 2 Tb.)*
- *24 oz. unbleached white flour (5 cups – 2 Tb.)*
- *1 Tb. sea salt*
- *1 tsp. instant yeast (page 24) (1½ tsp. dry yeast)*
- *2½ cups water, anywhere from body temperature to 120°F (48°C)*
- *1 Tb. caraway seeds*

Knead the above ingredients very thoroughly. As with the Basic French Bread recipe, allow 12 hours for the first rising. The dough at the start should be a little more moist than the French. The chopped rye absorbs moisture so that 12 hours later you will have a dough that holds a round shape. Make sure that the dough is tough enough to hold a nice round shape as well as having the proper sour moisture to make a long-lasting bread.

After the 12-hour rise, shape the dough into two balls and cover. Allow the 2 balls to rise for 2–4 hours or until double in size.

This bread sometimes takes its time in rising the second time. You must be patient!

Covering the round loaves will keep the surface moist and soft especially on dry winter days. This process is called proofing when put in a warm place. To avoid an ugly, cracked finished loaf, you must proof it. If you cannot avoid the tough dry skin, brush on an egg glaze. Sprinkle poppy seeds on it before slicing a checkered pattern on the top of the loaves. (Make the egg glaze by beating a whole egg or egg yolk with water. Paint it on with a pastry brush or new paint brush.)

Cook for 40 minutes at 350°F (170°C) until the bottom is brown and crisp. You can bake a crusty bread, but for a longer-lasting moist bread cook it lightly. Crusty or moist, it slices best when cooled thoroughly.

To make Onion Sourdough Rye you must be careful to take away 1 tablespoon of water for the ¼ cup of sliced onions that you add to the recipe. The moisture of the onions makes a less resilient dough without the reduction of water.

This recipe calls for unbleached white flour. If you are interested in substituting whole wheat flour, see the recipes for Lenten and Maur's Rye.

Sour Wheat Barley (Whole Wheat French)

Like the Sourdough Rye, this bread has variations. In this case mix ½ pound of Basic French Bread dough (page 35) into the recipe below. For a simpler version just add ¼ pound white flour with an additional ¼ cup of water, or simply follow the recipe as is and get a richer whole wheat taste. Mixing in already kneaded and risen Basic French Bread dough is a rewarding endeavor incorporating the benefits of already risen dough and making a lighter bread.

- *1 lb. whole wheat (1 to 1 ratio with cracked wheat optional) (3 cups)*
- *1 lb. unbleached white flour (3¼ cups)*
- *1 tsp. instant yeast (page 24) (1½ tsp. dry yeast)*
- *1 Tb. sea salt*
- *½ cup barley (cooked 5–10 minutes)*
- *2 cups + 2 Tb. water, anywhere from body temperature to 120°F (48°C)*

Knead all the above ingredients with or without the additional flour and water or the ½ pound Basic French Bread dough. Allow the dough to rise for 12 hours in a closed container. Cut into 2 pieces to make round breads. Place on a cornmealed pan to rise for several more hours (3–4) before baking at 350°F (175°C) for 40 minutes. An egg glaze can be applied and topped with various seeds.

We also use this dough to make a whole wheat French. Cut the dough into pieces and roll out into French bread shapes. Place on cornmealed trays or floured canvases. (See Basic French Bread, page 29, for instructions.)

Poppy Louis

(makes 2 loaves)

- 2 lb. unbleached white flour (6½ cups)
- 4 oz. whole wheat flour (¾ cup)
- 4 oz. Rye Mix (page 40) (¾ cup)
- ½ cup poppy seeds
- 2⅔ cups water, anywhere from body temperature to 120°F (48°C)
- 1½ Tb. sea salt
- 1 tsp. instant yeast (page 24)
- extra poppy seeds for topping

Knead all the above ingredients together until a smooth, elastic poppy-seeded dough ball emerges which will spring back. Put into a container for the first 12-hour rising with the temperature at 68°F.

Then take this piece or several pieces of dough and roll into round loaves. Grab the round loaf by pinching it with the tip of your fingers from the top and submerge the bottom half in water. Dab this wet half in a bowl full of poppy seeds. Carefully put the loaf on a cornmealed pan with the poppy seed topping facing up.

Place the tray next to or above the stove and allow a rising of twice the volume which may be as long as 3 hours.

Bake for 40 minutes at 350°F (175°C). Home ovens are generally hotter than commercial ovens. Therefore the bread may be done in 30 minutes. In order to simulate a larger oven, preheat the oven to 450°F and reduce to 350°F as soon as the bread is in the oven.

Pumpernickel

(may make two 2-pound loaves)

pumpernickel (pum´per-nik´el).
A coarse slightly sour bread made with unbolted rye.
Random House Dictionary

There is a story that during Napoleon's campaign through Prussia he was handed a loaf of this rye bread and remarked: "Ça c´est bon pour Nickel" (his white horse). Perhaps a slight German modification of this quote accounts for the origin of this name.

Make a batch of Sourdough Rye (page 42). Just after the dough is mixed and before the 12-hour rising, add the following and mix until homogeneous. If chopped rye is not available, coarsely ground rye berries or rye flakes will suffice.

- *½ lb. chopped rye soaked in ½ cup water for 1 hour*
- *⅓ cup dark molasses*
- *1 Tb. cocoa powder*

Allow to rise for 12 hours before forming into 2 round loaves to be placed on a tray sprinkled with cornmeal. After they have doubled in size, bake for 40 minutes at 350°F (170°C). This bread is moist and delicious.

When temperatures exceed 80°F (27°C), the pumpernickel may flatten while rising on the trays and decrease in volume while baking. You may compensate for the sagging and the shrinking by decreasing the water for soaking the chopped rye to ¼ cup instead of ½ cup. If the temperature and moisture are extreme (90°F, 32°C), eliminate the ½ cup of water altogether. The results will be a larger round loaf with the same qualities but showing more chopped rye in the texture.

Lenten Bread

(makes four 1½-pound loaves)

This recipe was devised to be made during Lent for those desiring to eat no animal products from Ash Wednesday through Easter. This bread will compliment vegetable sandwiches or vegetable stews and soups.

- *1¾ lb. (28 oz.) Rye Mix (page 40) (5¼ cups)*
- *1 lb. whole wheat flour (3⅓ cups)*
- *4½ cups water, anywhere from body temperature to 120°F (48°C)*
- *1 Tb. ground or pulverized wakame seaweed (arame, hiziki, or kombu may also be used)*
- *1 Tb. caraway seeds*

Mix and allow to sit covered overnight for about 12 hours. Some natural fermentation should start in order to give it its sour taste. During cool weather, place the mix in a warm spot. Remember no yeast is allowed in this portion.

Twelve hours later mix in 1½ pounds Basic French Bread dough which has also risen for the 12 hours. Here is half the Basic French Bread recipe given on page 29, which will give the 1½ pounds needed for this recipe.

- *1 lb. wheat flour (unbleached white or whole)*
- *1 cup + 1 Tb. water*
- *1 tsp. instant yeast (page 24)*
- *½ Tb. sea salt (optional)*

Mix and allow to rise along side the other portion for 12 hours. As long as there is good yeast activity, doughs that have been frozen or made of whole wheat will work fine for the Lenten bread.

Now combine the two doughs and mix them thoroughly. If you have no mixer, your hands will be very pasty. After the two doughs are mixed, put the dough in pans and, after a 15-minute rest, place in the oven. This dough will not hold a shape therefore the dough must be put in a pan. Do not be bothered if the dough doesn't rise very much. This is not a light bread. Cook slowly in an oven at 300–350°F (160°C) for 90 minutes.

This recipe makes approximately three 2-pound or four 1½-pound loaves. Lenten Bread is very good when it has just cooled off. This bread tastes even better when it is a day old and can be cut paper-thin. It keeps for weeks in a refrigerator.

Carababa

(makes 2 loaves)

- 2 lb. unbleached white flour (6½ cups)
- 4 oz. whole wheat flour (¾ cup)
- 4 oz. Rye Mix (page 40) (¾ cup)
- ¼ cup caraway seeds
- 2½ cups water, anywhere from body temperature to 120°F (48°C)
- 1½ Tb. sea salt
- 1 tsp. instant yeast (page 24) (1½ tsp. dry yeast)
- extra caraway seeds for topping

Knead all the above ingredients together until a smooth caraway-specked dough can be balled up. Put the dough into a covered container for a 12-hour rise (similar rising to the Basic French Bread). Then cut the dough into two pieces and roll into round loaves. Grab the round loaf by pinching it with the tip of your fingers from the top and submerge the bottom half in water. Then press this wet half into the caraway seeds.

Carefully put the loaf on a cornmealed pan with the caraway seed topping facing up. Allow a rising of twice the volume, which may be as long as 3 hours, before baking for 40 minutes at 350°F (175°C).

Open Sesame (à la Baba)

(makes 2 loaves)

This is a soured yeast recipe and can be made directly from the other sour yeast bread recipes or from the one given here. The one thing crucial to this recipe is to make sure the sesame seeds are roasted. Sesame seeds are not often sold roasted so it will require roasting some ahead. The sesame seeds should be taken out of the oven when lightly browned. (Darker roasted seeds are also good if that is your preference.) The sesame taste is present throughout and the crust has a crackly surface for the first day.

- *1 lb. whole wheat flour (3 cups)*
- *1 lb. unbleached white flour (3¼ cups)*
- *1 tsp. instant yeast (page 24) (1½ tsp. dry yeast)*
- *1½ Tb. sea salt*
- *2 cups + 2 Tb. water, anywhere from body temperature to 120°F (48°C)*
- *½ lb. roasted sesame seeds, hulled or unhulled (¾ cup)*

Set the sesame seeds aside. Mix the flour, yeast, water, and salt until a nice firm ball of dough is formed. Place in a covered container to rise for 12 hours. When the 12 hours are up, knead in the roasted sesame seeds. Cut the dough in 2 and roll each piece of dough into a ball by stretching the top outside surface and tucking the side edges underneath while pinching the bottoms of the loaves together with the 2 outer edges of your palms. Set on a tray sprinkled with cornmeal and allow 2–4 hours for the loaves to double in bulk. They will look like water balloons on a flat surface. Egg-glaze the top of the crust, if you wish, and sprinkle the top with roasted sesame seeds. Slice the top with a knife or razor blade in the form of a flapping wing or any other design.

Cook for about 40 minutes at 375°F (190°C); the bread will acquire a dark crisp crust in an oven at 450°F (230°C). Regardless of how the outside looks, the inside of the bread must be allowed to cook. The bottom of the bread knows best how to tell you if the bread is cooked through. Tapping on the bottom and hearing a hollow sound is the true indicator of the bread being done.

The Braid or The Wreath

(Makes two braids or wreaths with diameters of approximately 12 inches)

Make two batches of Basic French Bread (page 35) and one batch of the straight Sourdough Rye (page 42).

- *1 batch Basic French Bread plain*
- *1 batch Basic French Bread mixed with:*

    2 cup grated cheese

    4 Tb. parsley

    4 Tb. dry chives

    4 tsp. garlic powder

    4 tsp. Herb Mix (page 73)

- *1 batch Sourdough Rye*

Allow the doughs to rise separately for 12 hours. Knock down the doughs. Cut the 3 kinds of dough in half. Roll out into 3 different strands, each about 2 feet long. Do this again with the other 3 halves.

Lay the 3 different strands side-by-side and cross the middle strand over one of the side strands. Then take the new middle strand and lay it over the other side strand and so on. When the three strands are totally braided, you may connect the three ends together. Conceal the connection with a small bow made of a piece of the rye.

Place the braid on a cornmealed tray and allow to swell to 3 times its size. Paint egg-glaze on the cheese-herb French and rye strands, leaving the plain French unglazed. Place poppy seeds on the rye and sesame seeds on the cheese-herb French. Bake at 350°F (175°C) until brown and crisp on the bottom.

The Sour Wheat Barley (page 44) can be used in place of one of the strands.

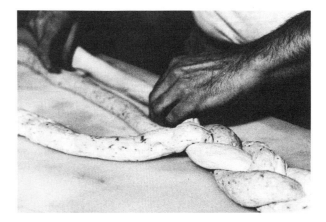

Walnut Bread

(makes 2 loaves)

The walnuts transform this bread. The bread has a glow when baked and any walnuts sticking out on the surface of the bread are crisp and delicious. The nut taste is present in the whole bread, and there is a sweetness in this bread because of the walnuts.

This is a soured yeast bread and can be made directly from leftover Sour Wheat Barley dough as well as the Basic French Bread dough. (Check the Walnut Bread in the "Hall of Receipts.")

Any naturally leavened sourdough may be added, not to exceed ⅓ of the whole.

- *1 lb. whole wheat flour (3 cups)*
- *1 lb. unbleached white flour (3¼ cups)*
- *1 tsp. instant yeast (page 24) (1½ tsp. dry yeast)*
- *1½ Tb. sea salt*
- *2 cups + 2 Tbs. water, anywhere from body temperature to 120°F (48°C)*
- *½ lb. walnut halves and pieces (2 rounded cups)*

Knead together all the above (except the walnuts) to get an homogeneous firm ball. Place in a covered container and allow 12 hours rising time in temperate conditions (70°F, 22°C).

At the end of 12 hours, mix the walnuts into the dough. When the walnuts are well kneaded in, the new dough will acquire a pink or mauve color.

Cut the new dough in half and roll each piece of dough into a ball by stretching the top outside surface and tucking the side edges underneath while pinching the bottom of the loaves together with the two outer edges of one's palms. Walnut pieces will break out through the surface.

Set on a tray sprinkled with cornmeal and allow 2–4 hours for the loaves to double their size and acquire a smooth surface (aside from the walnuts). Then egg-glaze the crust. On the top surface, cut slices with a knife or razor blade in the form of a flapping wing.

Cook for 40 minutes at 375°F (190°C). I need to emphasize that it is impossible to know how long it will take to cook this bread in your oven. My 40 minutes cooking time is only good as an approximation. Cooking this bread in a hotter oven (450°F, 230°C) for less time will give a crisp outside with a nutty moist inside. The bread is cooked when a light brown crisp bottom sounds hollow to the tapping of the fingers. This bread ages well.

Peter's Grain Bread

(makes 2 loaves)

This dough will result in a softer and less crispy crusted bread.

Cook ⅓ cup of millet in ⅔ cup of water. Gently boil for about 10 minutes and allow it to cool.

☞ Soak for ½ hour:

- *1⅓ cups oatmeal*
- *⅔ cup bulgur wheat*
- *1 cup wheat flakes*
- *⅔ cup sunflower seeds*
- *¼ cup molasses*
- *1 cup water, anywhere from body temperature to 120°F (48°C)*

☞ Knead all the ingredients below:

- *1 lb. whole wheat flour (3 cups)*
- *1 lb. unbleached white flour (3¼ cups)*
- *1 tsp. instant yeast (page 24) (1½ tsp. dry yeast)*
- *1 Tb. sea salt*
- *2 cups + 2 Tb. water, anywhere from body temperature to 120°F (48°C)*

Mix the dough, the soaked grain, and the cooked millet until it has an even color. Set it in a covered container and allow it to rise for 12 hours. Note that the dough will be more spongy than the other soured yeast breads.

Divide the dough in half and make 2 round loaves. Place them on a tray sprinkled with cornmeal and allow to rise for 2–4 hours more. Bake at 350°F (175°C) for 40 minutes or until the bottoms have a crisp surface and a hollow sound when tapped with the fingers.

The only way to pass any test,
is to take the test. It is inevitable.

Chief Regal Black Swan
from Mutant Message
by Marlo Morgan

Naturally Leavened Breads

Levin, leaven, leven, and au levain all mean the same thing, and naturally leavened will be used here to describe dough fermenting of itself without the addition of yeast.

There are rumors going around that claim that yeast breads, in particular whole wheat yeast breads, have a decalcifying effect when inside the intestines. It is important to point out that there are different chemistries between yeast bread and naturally leavened bread. Yeast doughs enhance the presence of phytates (phytic acids) which are in the wheat germ and are activated by the yeast and which bind up minerals. More digestible naturally leavened bread contains phytase which counteracts the phytates and thus allows the intestines to assimilate more of these oligoelements.

It was found by M. Boulanger that yeast breads had 85 percent phytates for 4 hours rising time and 60 percent for 8 hours rising time. Some of the yeast recipes in this book, which call for as much as 16 hours of rising time, should reduce the presence of phytates even more, bringing the phytate level closer to that of naturally leavened breads, which were recorded at 10 percent and 15 percent for the same rising times.

This quotation by Antoine Bosse Platiere will give you more comparisons: "I would say that the yeast utilized in bread-making has a little bit of the image of our industrial societies: prolific and uniform, invading and imperialistic (incorporated in a leavened dough, the yeast will take the upper hand over the other fermenters), drunk with speed and with performance, qualitywise impoverished . . ."

It is important to note that not all is known about the yeast and naturally leavened doughs. The simple fact is that naturally leavened dough comes about spontaneously so to speak (flour, water, and air mixed). It has a particular flavor and for this reason it is worthy of experimentation. The ancients used to experiment by adding leavened grains from beer making and the foam from wine vats to their dough to promote the bread rising.

There is no reason why natural fermentations such as soured grains (soaked, leftover, cooked, and sprouted) and hardened juices and cider (no preservative) can't be effective tools to leaven bread.

Naturally leavened bread is time-consuming, which makes it difficult to produce on short notice. The way to get around this schedule is to have naturally leavened dough on hand at all times and to mix it with yeast doughs. This is not a new idea, but it is something I discovered with the Lenten Bread (page 47) and the Six Grain and One Bean Bread (page 76). At times I added naturally leavened dough in with the Walnut Bread (page 52) as well as other yeast bread recipes. Mixing yeast dough with up to a third naturally leavened dough can maintain some of the flavor and moisture of a naturally leavened bread while enjoying the shorter times and lighter texture of a yeast bread.

Once the naturally leavened dough is established, keeping a portion of this dough aside as starter to introduce into the next batch of bread is helpful for those making bread daily (see Everyday Sourdough Bread, page 64). In the case of the Three-Day Sourdough Bread recipe (page 58), no starter is required and no dough needs to be saved.

Three-Day Sourdough Bread

(makes 2 or 3 loaves)

This is one of the oldest bread recipes in history. The origin of bread as food, its sacred beginning and its hidden secrets, are in the ingredients of this bread—flour, water, salt, and time. Before the advent of commercial yeast, there were only these kinds of naturally leavened breads. This bread ages well. In the open it keeps its flavor and moisture inside and its crispness on the outside.

This naturally leavened bread has a greater density than a yeast bread; its crust is thicker and more crisp; its inside is more irregular and elastic. It can be cut very thin and, most of all, it has a tangy taste very hard to imitate with a yeast bread.

The natural yeast that appears spontaneously out of the wheat itself is more subtle than a commercial yeast. It is a simple process to make this bread as long as some natural fermentation begins in the first day's mix (starter) and you take the full 3 days needed.

The name, Three-Day Sourdough Bread, describes the process and helps distinguish this bread from the over-used term "sourdough" that people have given yeast breads which are not real sourdough breads. Real sourdough breads are naturally fermented breads such as this one using no yeast. (The soured yeast breads in this book gain their sourdoughlike tang from the 12-hour rise of the dough.)

This dough is intentionally made firm in order to avoid a flat saucer shape that occurs when the dough is too moist. The firmness also helps control the souring especially during hot spells when daily temperatures reach 80–90°F (26–32°C). The souring of the dough makes each daily step easier as the dough gets more gentle and soft.

It is essential to start the first day with whole wheat flour. White flour sours but lacks the flavor. In the second and third days, use a mix of the whole wheat and the unbleached white wheat flours to get a higher rise and smoother texture.

Table for Three-Day Bread

This recipe will take 3 full days from start to finish. Measuring with cups is not accurate. You need to weigh the ingredients, then transfer them into cups. If the results of your measuring matches the weight of the preceding chart, the dough will be perfect. Total weight of dough: 4¼ pounds.

	Procedure	Flour	Water	Salt	Time
Day 1	Preparation of the starter: Mix ingredients	◆ 1 pound of whole wheat flour (3 cups)	1 cup	none	Rest 24 hours
Day 2	Preparation of the leavened dough: Add above mixture to these ingredients and knead	◆ ¼ pound whole wheat (¾ cup) ◆ ¾ pound white	1 cup	1 Tb.	Rest 24 hours
Day 3	Final preparation: Add above to these ingredients and knead	◆ ¼ pound whole wheat (¾ cup) ◆ ¾ pound white flour (2¼ cups)	1 cup	none	Rest 20 hours
	Shape loaves				Rest 4 hours or more

Tools

☞ For mixing:

◆ *Hand kneading is recommended unless you have a strong commercial mixer. The dough must be tough especially in first two steps*

☞ For rising:

◆ *a plastic container with cover or bowl (covered) or a plastic bag*

☞ For cooking:

◆ *a cookie sheet or pan*
◆ *a small amount of cornmeal*
◆ *a sharp knife*
◆ *an oven at 450°F (240°C)*
◆ *a little water to throw in the oven for steam*

The Procedure

☞ Day 1

Mix 1 pound of whole wheat with 1 cup of warm water using your hands until all the flour is incorporated. Place in a covered container.

At the end of the first 24 hours, the dough should feel slightly spongy when touched and have a slight increase in volume of 25 percent. If you use a plastic bag and you notice condensation above the bread inside the bag, this is a good sign indicating that the dough is fermenting.

☞ Day 2

In the second step, mix the first step's dough with 1 cup of water, ¼ pound of whole wheat, ¾ pound of unbleached white flour and 1 tablespoon of salt. Using your hands again to give it a thorough mix. Allow a temperate 24-hour rest to this piece of dough.

During the extreme hot weather (80°–90°F, 26–32°C) you may add 1 teaspoon more salt and a tiny bit less water (1 tablespoon); you will then have, at the worst, a well soured bread.

The whole second step may be kept in the refrigerator. It is also on this second day that you can postpone the process for a few days by leaving it in the refrigerator the whole time. Then, from the refrigerator, you can proceed with the third day of kneading (third step).

☞ Day 3

For the third step, incorporate the dough from the second step with 1 cup of water, ¼ pound of whole wheat, and ¾ pounds of unbleached white flour until it is homogeneous.

Allow a 20-hour rest for the third and final rise. At the end of the third step, divide the dough into 2 or 3 pieces and roll into round or slightly oblong loaves. It should require almost no flour as the dough is not overly sticky.

Set the 2 or 3 loaves on a cornmealed pan and allow them a 4-hour rest or more. A longer rise (as much as 8 hours) may be necessary in colder conditions if the dough seems to be slow in rising. The rising loaves will spread to some degree no matter how firm. When cooking, the breads will expand up to 3 times their prebaked height.

Covering the rising loaves for the 4-hour rise with a bowl, bucket, or plastic bag keeps the surface moist and will enhance rising and crispness. Wetting the inside of the bowl that covers the rising loaves is recommended.

Using a sharp knife or razor, slice deep crosses in the top of the bread in order to avoid side hernias and to release any large air holes that may develop on the upper part of the loaf.

☞ Baking

Cook in a hot oven at 450°F for no less than 30 minutes (for home ovens). A tablespoon of water thrown into the oven alongside the bread but not on the bread makes steam to give an extra eggshell crackle to the crust.

Shaping of the 2 or 3 loaves on a cornmealed tray is very important. Allow the loaves the full 4 hours rest while covered. Slice crosses or X's in the top of the loaf. Rest 4 hours. Place in a hot oven (450°F, 240°C) for 30–40 minutes.

Everyday Sourdough Bread

This is a true sourdough bread. When this soured bread comes out of the oven, it smells sour like brewed grain. It is difficult to find this bread. This is not because it is difficult to make but because it takes up space and time. Commercially it has been abandoned. We make but a small amount daily (thus the name). It starts like the Three-Day Sourdough Bread. It differs only in that we keep it going by extracting a portion (the starter) each time we make bread, and thus save ourselves 2 full days in the process.

This recipe is ideal for those who can use a few loaves of bread on a daily basis. The key here is the length of time the dough rises before it goes into the oven. This process lasts 15 hours. It does particularly well when the temperature is 60–70°F (16–20°C). All dough when it is not allowed to rise for a long enough time or if it overrises will turn into a brick after it is cooked. This brick could be used as a doorstop or a paperweight. I make an effort to avoid the bricks—they don't sell well. I time the final rising process, so crucial to the success of this bread, so that it occurs during the night.

This recipe will make six 1½-pound loaves of bread. If you desire more or less, you will need to divide or multiply proportionally.

☞ Step 1:

Mix 2 pounds of whole wheat flour with 2 cups of water. Let it sit for 24 hours. Between 60° and 70°F (16–20°C) are ideal temperatures.

☞ Step 2:

Mix this dough with 2 pounds of whole wheat flour and 2 cups of water. Let it sit for another 24 hours. There should be visible fermenting activity. The dough should look as if it is being inflated. The impression is that of a thin skin pumped full of air bubbles. If the dough is not rising and it is glossy or if there are pink or red spots in the dough, don't bother with it; discard it and start over. This happens occasionally. This doesn't result from not doing something you were supposed to do, it just happens.

☞ Step 3:

At the end of this second 24-hour rest, cut the dough in two; this yields 2 portions of 3¾ pounds each. To one portion add 2 pounds of whole wheat and 2 cups of water and put aside for another day. This first portion can be cut in half again the next day and the process outlined below repeated. Thus the process can go on indefinitely.

◆

☞ To the second portion of dough, add 2 pounds of whole wheat flour, 2 pounds of unbleached white flour, 4 cups of water, 2 tablespoons of salt, and mix well. Allow this portion to set about 4 hours and then form into loaves; they can be round- or oblong-shaped, or they can be put in tin loaf pans. They should be allowed 15 hours to rise before putting them in the oven. The loaves should blow up to double their volumes.

The 15-hour rising period is for temperatures in the 60°–70°F (16–20°C) range. The rising time can be less for the 75°–90°F (24–32°C) temperature range. All the steps can be delayed especially if the dough is put in a cool spot.

Traditionally these breads were put in canvas-lined baskets for a long rise, and then turned out to be put into big ovens. In this recipe you may do this. But why disturb the dough needlessly and possibly cause the falling of the dough? Place the loaves for the final rise on a cornmealed or floured pan. Allow the full rise in the loaf pan or on the sheet pan on which you intend to cook the breads.

Cook the bread at 370°F (190°C) until the bottom sounds hollow. If the bread has risen well, it will not expand much more during the baking time. Slices on the top are optional.

Alain's Essene Bread (Uncle Al's Cake)

This bread or pan bread was created without any previous knowledge of what was done in Egypt or Israel. This bread was made with the aid of an electric food processor. Eating sprouted wheat raw (or just cooked into mush) was the first step to discovering this bread now, as well as in ancient times.

Mashing sprouted wheat in a food processor makes a sweet dough. If the sprout is about as long as the kernel then the moisture will be about right. Note that the sprout is not the fuzzy white tail that first comes out but the green shoot that comes out later. If the sprout becomes longer and greenish, you will have a more moist mush that would require some flour to thicken the dough.

This bread can be fried in a pan, but you can also cook it in an oven. The pan bread is best when there is a crispy crust on the outside and the middle is still glutinous and moist.

If the blended sprout dough is not used that same day, it will sour and become a leavened dough. The sweetness will fade and a sweet and sour quality will take its place.

Blend 2 cups of sprouted wheat (with sprouts as long as kernels) in a food processor or an old, mechanical meat grinder until a thick, gluteny dough ball is formed. These doughs may be used right away, or they may sit and sour.

When the patty-forming dough is ready, lay it in your pan. With a small sprig of rosemary on the surface, fry or bake slowly until crisp to your liking. This bread is good to take on a camping trip.

If the sprouts are too long, the dough will be juicy. This juiciness is caused by wheat grass juice and must be compensated for with flour.

☞ For a juicy sprout bread, mix the following:

- *2 cups sprouted wheat*
- *10 oz. whole wheat flour (2 cups)*
- *¾ cup water*

A kindly thought sent out
toward some other human being is
a protection to that other, and it
is a beautiful thing to do. It is a
human thing, a truly human
thing, and one that every normal
human being loves to do.

Gift of the Lotus
compiled by Virginia Hanson

Yeast Breads

Oat Bran Bread

(makes 2 loaves)

Combining oatmeal in an oat bran bread has a taste that you can't get with oat bran alone.

- *2 lb. unbleached white flour (6½ cups)*

  (optional: substitute 6 cups whole wheat for white flour)
- *1 tsp. instant yeast (page 24) (1½ tsp. dry yeast)*
- *1 tsp. sea salt*
- *2 Tb. soy flour*
- *¼ cup wheat bran*
- *2 Tb. oil*
- *3 cups water, anywhere from body temperature to 120°F (48°C)*
- *1 cup oatmeal*
- *1½ cup oat bran*
- *2 Tb. molasses (optional)*

Set aside the 1 cup of oatmeal and mix all of the above. When well mixed, knead in remaining 1 cup of oatmeal. The dough will be sticky, but the moisture will be absorbed by the oatmeal. After the first rising of as much as 3 hours and an additional 1-hour rise in 2 oiled pans, bake at 350°F (175°C) for 40 minutes.

Oatmeal Bread

(makes 2 loaves)

- *2 lb. unbleached white flour (6½ cups)*
  (optional: substitute 6 cups whole wheat for white flour)
- *1 tsp. instant yeast (page 24) (1½ tsp. dry yeast)*
- *1 tsp. sea salt*
- *2 Tb. soy flour*
- *¼ cup wheat bran or oat bran*
- *2 Tb. oil*
- *3 cups water, anywhere from body temperature to 120°F (48°C)*
- *2 cups oatmeal*
- *2 Tb. molasses (optional)*

Set aside 1 cup of oatmeal and mix all of the above. When well mixed, knead in the remaining 1 cup of oatmeal. The dough will be sticky, but the moisture will be absorbed by the oatmeal. After the first rising of as much as 3 hours and an additional 1-hour rise in 2 oiled pans, bake at 350°F (175°C) for 40 minutes.

Cornmeal Oat Bran Bread

This bread is for those who want no wheat and no dairy. Soy milk gives a lighter texture. If you use dairy milk , add 2 teaspoons of vinegar to the milk.

- *2 eggs*
- *2 cups soy milk*
- *2 cups whole cornmeal*
- *1 cup oat bran*
- *1–2 tsp. baking soda*
- *1–2 tsp. baking powder*
- *½ tsp. salt (optional)*

Beat eggs lightly into soy milk and pour into dry ingredients. Mix and bake in an oiled pan or 2 at 350°F (175°C) until done, no more than 25 minutes. Less is best and let it cool.

Anadama Bread

(makes 2 loaves)

"Anna, damn her," said he of his wife when he had to make the bread.

- *2 lb. unbleached white flour (6½ cups) (optional: substitute whole wheat for all or a percentage of the white flour)*
- *1 tsp. instant yeast (page 24) (1½ tsp. dry yeast)*
- *1 tsp. sea salt*
- *4 Tb. soy flour*
- *¼ cup wheat bran*
- *¼ cup oil*
- *½ cup cornmeal (whole with germ)*
- *2½ cups water, anywhere from body temperature to 120°F (48°C)*
- *¼ cup blackstrap molasses*

Knead all ingredients together well. Allow to rise for 3 hours. Knock down, cut in 2, and put in oiled pans for a second rising of an hour or until double in bulk. Bake the loaves at 350°F (175°C) for 40 minutes.

Cheese Herb Bread

(makes 2 loaves)

Attention! There is no cheese too foul-smelling or moldy to use in this bread. This bread will vary according to the condition, quantities, and kinds of cheese. Yeast activities may be affected by moldy cheese (blue mold). Fresh herbs and garlic will enhance your bread.

White bread may be made from this recipe by omitting the herbs, garlic powder, and cheese.

- *2 lb. unbleached white flour (or whole wheat) (6½ cups)*
- *1–2 tsp. instant yeast (page 24) (1½ tsp. dry yeast)*
- *1 tsp. sea salt*
- *3 Tb. soy flour*
- *⅓ cup wheat bran (unless using whole wheat)*
- *⅓ cup oil*
- *1 Tb. dry or fresh chives*
- *1 Tb. dry or fresh parsley*
- *¾ tsp. garlic powder*
- *2 tsp. Herb Mix*
- *⅛ –¼ lb. or more grated cheese (mozzarella is used in our bakeries)*
- *2½ cups water, anywhere from body temperature to 120°F (48°C)*

Mix everything all at once. Cheese, if firm, should be grated. If it's ripe and soft, it should be kneaded until well incorporated into the dough. Allow to rise for 3 hours; divide in 2 for a second rising of an hour inside the 2 oiled pans. Bake for 40 minutes at 350°F (175°C).

For whole wheat substitution, the water may have to be increased to 3 cups with longer kneading required.

Herb Mix

The following weight-volume proportions are approximations.

- *1 lb. basil (12 cups)*
- *¼ lb. marjoram (3 cups)*
- *¼ lb. thyme (3 cups)*
- *¼ lb. savory (3 cups)*
- *¼ lb. rosemary (3 cups)*
- *¼ lb. sage (3 cups)*
- *½ cup oregano*

Raisin Bread

(makes 2 loaves)

This is the messiest bread we make. It is the only bread we make that has sugar in it. The brown sugar will overflow while the bread is cooking. A small sheet pan under the bread pan will keep your oven free of carbonized sugar.

- *2 lb. unbleached white flour (6½ cups)*
- *1 tsp. instant yeast (page 24) (1½ tsp. dry yeast)*
- *1 tsp. sea salt*
- *2 Tb. soy flour*
- *¼ cup wheat bran (with or without the germ or plain wheat germ)*
- *4 Tb. oil*
- *½ cup or more raisins*
- *2½ cups water, anywhere from body temperature to 120°F (48°C)*

☞ To be used for the swirl:

- *2 Tb. melted butter*
- *1 Tb. cinnamon*
- *1–2 cups brown sugar*

Mix all dry ingredients, oil, and water until well kneaded. After the first rising of 2–3 hours, make 2 flat rectangles about 7 × 12 inches. Paint the surface with melted butter, leaving a margin unbuttered on the sides. Sprinkle the whole surface with cinnamon. On top of the butter and cinnamon, spread the brown sugar. One-half cup of brown sugar per loaf is adequate. The amount of brown sugar used is left to the baker's discretion.

Roll up the 7-inch side like a rug and tuck in the edges. The dough should be such that the seams stick and seal and minimize the escaping brown sugar-butter-cinnamon mixture.

Allow to rise about 1 hour and put in a 350°F (175°C) oven for about 40 minutes. The melted sugar spiral will often overflow. When done, tip breads upside down on a drip pan and remove the bread pans.

Restaurants are using this bread to make French toast, also referred to as the "breakfast bread." It is only fair to state that 3 toasters, that we know of, have been incinerated by toasting this bread.

Six Grain and One Bean (Seven Grain)

(makes 2 or 3 loaves)

☞ Soak overnight:

- *½ cup oatmeal*
- *¼ cup cracked wheat*
- *¼ cup bulgar wheat*
- *¼ cup Rye Mix flour (page 40)*
- *¼ cup soy flour*
- *¼ cup barley*
- *¼ cup millet*
- *¼ cup whole cornmeal*
- *1 cup sprouted wheat or alfalfa sprouts (with ½-inch white tails)*
- *1 cup water*

Soaked grain often ferments naturally to give a sour grain taste.

☞ Mix in the soaked grains with the following:

- *2½ lb. whole wheat flour (7½ cups)*
- *2 Tb. oil*
- *1 tsp. sea salt*
- *1 tsp. instant yeast (page 24) (1½ tsp. dry yeast)*
- *2¼ cups water, anywhere from body temperature to 120°F (48°C)*

Knead this mixture. It is impossible to overknead this bread. If using an electric mixer, let it mix for 10 minutes or more.

Place the dough in a warm place to rise for at least 2 hours. In 3 oiled loaf pans, let the dough rise again before cooking it in a 350°F (175°C) oven for about 40 minutes. Make sure that the bread does not overrise in the pans or the bread will fall during cooking and not hold together well.

The same bread can be made by cooking the grain instead of soaking it overnight. Excluding the sprouts, bring the grain to a boil. Simmer for a few minutes and then allow to cool and add the sprouts. This works very well but there is no taste of the naturally fermented grain.

Swedish Rye (Limpa)

(makes 2 loaves)

- *1½ lb. unbleached white flour (5 cups – 2 Tb.)*
- *½ lb. Rye Mix (page 40) (1⅓ cups)*
- *1 tsp. instant yeast (page 24) (1½ tsp. dry yeast)*
- *½ to 1 tsp. cardamom powder*
- *1 tsp. sea salt*
- *½ cup orange juice*
- *4 Tb. oil*
- *¼ cup molasses*
- *1½ cups water, anywhere from body temperature to 120°F (48°C)*
- *melted butter*

Mix all the above ingredients, except the butter, until the dough is an even light brown color (molasses being well mixed in). Put in a closed container for 2 hours or whenever doubled in size.

Knock down the dough, cut it in half and place the 2 pieces into oiled loaf pans or form into round balls on a floured pan. Allow the 2 loaves to rise again until double in volume.

Brush the tops with butter just before placing in a 375°F (190°C) oven for 40 minutes.

After 30 minutes, check in intervals of a few minutes to gauge your own oven. The bread will be cooked when the bottom sounds hollow and when it springs back on top after being pressed gently with the tips of the fingers.

Sticky Buns

(makes approximately 24 buns)

☞ Dough:

- *2 lb. unbleached white flour (6½ cups)*
- *3 eggs*
- *1 tsp. instant yeast (page 24) (1½ tsp. dry yeast)*
- *½ cup sugar or maple syrup*
- *½ tsp. sea salt*
- *1½ cup water, anywhere from body temperature to 120°F (48°C)*
- *½ cup melted butter or margarine*

Place warm water in a bowl. Add salt, sweetener, yeast, and eggs, and beat lightly. Mix in flour and knead. Just when all the flour has been incorporated, add the melted butter and keep mixing until all the butter is worked in. Stop just before the dough begins to stick on the sides of the bowl. Place in an oiled plastic bag. Freeze for use on another day, or allow to rise to 3 times its volume. Pull out the night before use if it's frozen. This recipe will make 3½ pounds of dough.

☞ Filling:

- *¼ cup melted butter*
- *2–3 Tb. cinnamon*
- *3–4 cups brown sugar*
- *a handful of walnuts*
- *raisins (optional)*

Place the risen dough on a floured surface and roll out a rectangle of 30 × 20 inches. Paint the melted butter on the whole surface. Sprinkle the cinnamon on the buttered surface. Spread the brown sugar on the cinnamon. Walnuts can be placed on top of the brown sugar. Roll the long end up like a rug. Gently sway and stretch the roll until it is 48-inches long. Cut the roll into 2-inch cylinders and place the cylinders in an oiled cake or muffin tin.

Place the tins on a tray to catch overflowing brown sugar. Bake for 30 minutes at 350°F (175°C).

When taking the buns out of the oven, tip the muffin tins upside down on a drip rack over a pan and allow to cool. Excess melted brown sugar can be gathered and spread on the bottoms of the buns. These buns will be firm and will freeze well.

Fruit Fiber Bread

(makes 2 loaves)

☛ Wet Mixture (prepare ahead):

- *¾ cup frozen cranberries or soaked fresh cranberries (blueberries make a good substitute)*
- *¼ cup walnut pieces*
- *¼ cup chopped dates*
- *½ cup water to cook the above and then cool, or to soak 1 hour*

☛ Dry Mixture:

- *2¼ lb. unbleached white flour (7¼ cups)*
- *½ cup oatmeal*
- *½ cup oat bran*
- *¼ cup honey*
- *1 tsp. sea salt*
- *1 tsp. instant yeast (page 24) (1½ tsp. dry yeast)*
- *2 Tb. soy flour*
- *¼ cup wheat bran*
- *2 Tb. oil*
- *2 cups water, anywhere from body temperature to 120°F (48°C)*

Reserve ¼ cup frozen cranberries in a separate container to add at the end of the kneading to ensure whole pieces of cranberries in the mixed bread. If using whole fresh cranberries, it is important that the cranberries be split or made to burst by cooking to allow the bitter juices to seep into the dough.

Mix all the dry ingredients with the oil, the honey, and 2 cups water. Before the dough is completely mixed, pour in the wet mixture and knead thoroughly. To distribute the remaining ¼ cup of cranberries evenly in the dough, add them just before the mixing process is complete. The dates and the soaked cranberries will often disintegrate into the dough, creating a rich pink to purplish dough. The dough, at this point, should have a glossy look and a tacky consistency.

Allow the dough to rise until double in volume. Knock down the dough, shape and place into 2 oiled pans. Allow to rise again until double in size. Bake at 350°F (175°C) for 40 minutes. When cooked, the bread should resemble a moist cake. The bread is best when it has a moist consistency. This bread makes good toast.

Loaf Rye
(makes 2 loaves)

- *¾ lb. Rye Mix (page 40) (2 cups + 1 Tb.)*
- *1¼ lb. unbleached white flour (4 cups)*
- *1 tsp. instant yeast (page 24) (1½ tsp. dry yeast)*
- *1 tsp. sea salt*
- *2 Tb. soy flour*
- *¼ cup wheat bran*
- *¼ cup oil*
- *¼ cup blackstrap molasses*
- *¼ cup honey*
- *1 Tb. caraway seeds*
- *2¾ cups water, anywhere from body temperature to 120°F (48°C)*

Knead the above ingredients for a long time (10 minutes with mixer). It will be very sticky and puttylike. It should be fairly moist as the Rye Mix flour will absorb some of the moisture. Allow to rise for 3 hours. Cut and roll up dough and put in 2 oiled pans. Allow to rise again for 1 hour or until doubled in bulk before putting into oven at 350°F (175°C) for 40 minutes. One may egg-glaze the top of the loaf and sprinkle poppy seeds onto it before the baking.

I give the miracles I have
received.

A Course in Miracles

The Whole Wheats

Needless to say, whole wheats are not the most popular and are often neglected for lack of interest. Whole wheat flours also vary more than white flours. All this accounts for the one thing that must be stressed: you must knead this bread. If a mechanical mixer is available, put in a moderate load and allow to mix for 10–15 minutes. (Be very careful not to strain the mixer's motor.)

The first 3 recipes include adding ingredients after the first 3–4 hours of rising. This is to assure ultimate kneading before putting into oiled pans for the second and final rise before baking.

When we're talking whole wheat, we're talking kneading!

Whole Wheat Maple Walnut Bread

(makes 2 loaves)

- *2 lb. whole wheat flour (6 cups)*
- *1 tsp. instant yeast (page 24) (1½ tsp. dry yeast)*
- *1 tsp. sea salt*
- *1/4 cup oil*
- *3 cups water, anywhere from body temperature to 120°F (48°C)*

Knead the above ingredients for 10 minutes or more.

☞ Later add:

- *1 cup chopped walnuts*
- *½ cup maple syrup*

After a 3-hour rising, knead in the walnuts and maple syrup just before putting the loaves in oiled pans. After a good full pan is attained, bake at 350°F (175°C) for 40 minutes.

Date-Nut Whole Wheat Bread

(makes 2 loaves)

- *2 lb. whole wheat flour (6 cups)*
- *1 tsp. instant yeast (page 24) (1½ tsp. dry yeast)*
- *1 tsp. sea salt*
- *¼ cup oil*
- *3 cups water, anywhere from body temperature to 120°F (48°C)*

Knead the above ingredients for as long as 10–15 minutes.

☞ Later add:

- *1 cup pitted dates in ½ cup hot water or soaked overnight until soft*
- *½ cup diced walnuts*

Knead the whole wheat, yeast, salt, oil, and water and allow to rise for 3 hours. The dough should then be rekneaded with the dates and walnuts until nuts are evenly distributed. Allow to rise in 2 oiled pans and bake at 350°F (175°C) for 40 minutes.

Millet and Wheat Germ Whole Wheat Bread

(makes 2 loaves)

- *2 lb. whole wheat flour (6 cups)*
- *1 tsp. instant yeast (page 24) (1½ tsp. dry yeast)*
- *1 tsp. sea salt*
- *¼ cup oil*
- *3 cups water, anywhere from body temperature to 120°F (48°C)*

Knead the above ingredients for as long as 10–15 minutes.

☞ Later add:

- *1 cup millet*
- *½ cup wheat germ*

Knead millet and wheat germ into the dough after the first rising. Cut in 2 and place in oiled pans for second rising. Bake 40 minutes at 350°F (175°C).

Kim's Good Stuff

(makes 2 loaves)

- *2 lb. whole wheat flour (6 cups)*
- *1 tsp. instant yeast (page 24) (1½ tsp. dry yeast)*
- *1 tsp. sea salt*
- *¼ cup oil*
- *1 cup raisins*
- *⅔ cup sunflower seeds*
- *1 Tb. cinnamon*
- *3 cups water, anywhere from body temperature to 120°F (48°C)*
- *½ cup sesame seeds (optional)*

Mix all ingredients together for 10–15 minutes. Allow to rise well for 3–4 hours. Cut in 2 and put the pieces in oiled pans for the second rising. Allow them to rise and bulge out of the pans before baking at 350°F (175°C) for about 40 minutes. Dump pans when cooked and allow to cool.

So long as one feeds on
food from unhealthy soil,
the spirit will lack the stamina
to free itself from the prison
of the body.

Secrets of the Soil
by Rudolf Steiner

Croissants

Croissant Dough

(makes up to 4 dozen)

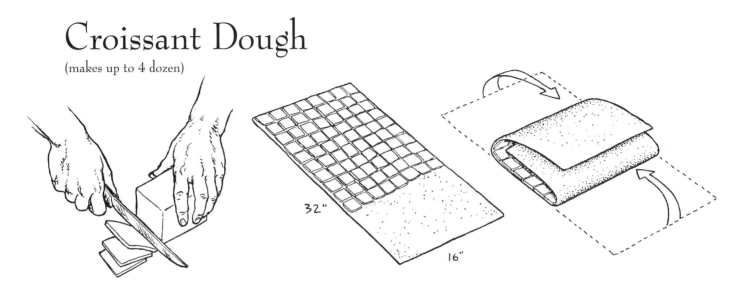

This croissant recipe is simple, although it does take 2–3 days to make. It requires slow rising, cooling, and long resting periods, following our method of letting doughs work on their own while we go about our business.

- *2½ lb. unbleached white flour (8 cups + 2 Tb.)*
- *1 Tb. sea salt*
- *1 tsp. instant yeast (page 24) (1½ tsp. dry yeast)*
- *2 cups water (body temperature)*
- *½ cup milk (cold)*
- *½ cup oil divided in half*

This recipe will make 4 dozen croissants with the option of making as few or as many of the 4 dozen as you wish, and freezing the rest. Freezing occurs early in the process and improves the croissants. The most rewarding results occur during cool weather. We do not recommend doing these croissants for the first time when it is around 90°F (32°C). It is the puffing (putting the butter onto the dough, folding, and rolling) that is the most temperature sensitive. The softness of the butter versus the toughness of the dough is the most crucial factor in making this recipe. As long as the croissant dough can be puffed in a cool environment, it will handle well later and cook up nicely even in a hot environment.

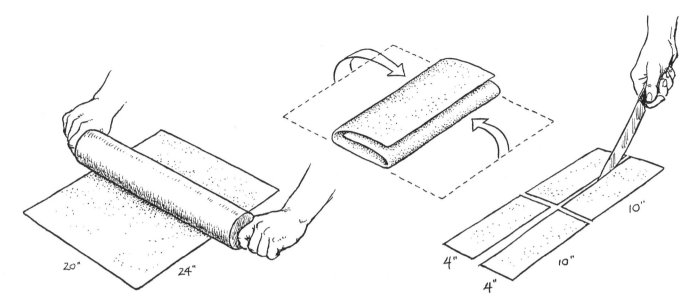

☛ For Puffing:

- *rolling pin*
- *large sharp knife*
- *1–½ lb. butter in solid block (unsalted if available)*

Put all the ingredients together, except the water and ¼ cup of the oil, and start mixing, adding water a little at a time. You should have some water and a ¼ cup of oil left to pick up all the crumbs and have a tough yet resilient dough. An electric mixer is a great advantage in adding water slowly. Put the dough in a covered container or plastic bag and refrigerate immediately. From the time the dough is refrigerated until it is ready to puff, 1–3 days later, the dough should have about doubled in volume. Most of the rising occurs in the first day; by the second or third day, due to refrigeration, the yeast activity is slowed down. This is why the dough has to be in a cool environment (39°F, 4°C) for those few days and kept in a covered container.

Overrising makes a tacky, soured dough that holds together poorly and makes a less flaky croissant in the end. In winter months, it may become necessary to soften the dough and enhance yeast activity. Enhancing the yeast and softening the dough is accomplished by increasing the quantities of warm liquid in increments of 2 tablespoons at a time. The recipe should give 4 pounds of dough.

91

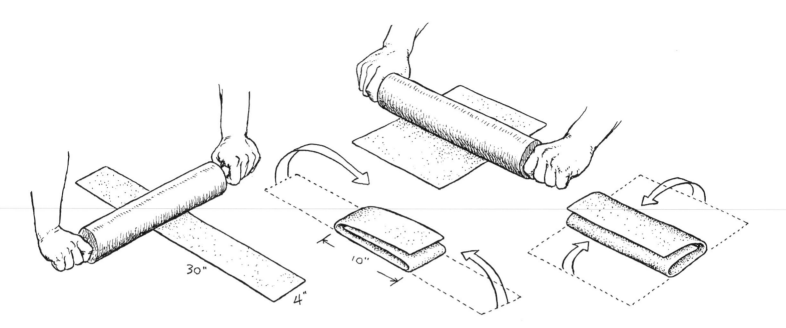

One or 2 days later, take the dough out of the refrigerator. The dough, to be ready, will have risen from 33 percent to 100 percent of its original volume. It will be more malleable but still tough. It is harder to work the tough dough, but the result is rewarding. Note that the dough will become easier to work as it nears its completion.

Roll out a rectangle 16 × 32 inches and cover ⅔ of the rectangle with fine (2 × 2 inches and ⅛ inch thick) slivers cut off the end of a 1-pound block of butter. Allow yourself ½ pound of extra butter to completely cover the ⅔ portion of the rectangle and to assure that there will be butter between all the layers of dough. Fold the ⅓ of the rectangle that is uncovered over half the covered portion, then fold the other covered half back over.

Next roll this rectangle out to about 20 × 24 inches and fold the long side into 3 again. Now cut in 4 with a cross to make four 4 × 10 inch pieces. Put 3 of the sections in the freezer. Leave 1 of the sections to rest in the refrigerator or a cold spot for 2–4 hours, at least, and overnight if convenient.

Pull the frozen pieces out the night before the day you want them and thaw them in the refrigerator. The croissant strips should be made into croissants within the same day. In the morning, take the 4 × 10 inch strip, roll it out to be 4 × 30 inches, then fold back in 3 to make a 4 × 10 inch piece again. Next, roll the other way to make a 10 × 12 inch piece. Fold the long side in 3 so that you

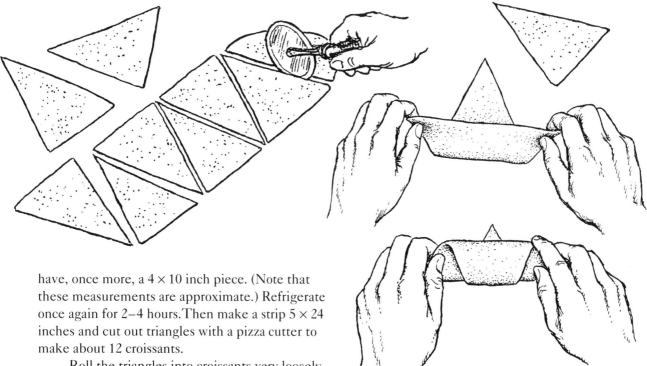

have, once more, a 4 × 10 inch piece. (Note that these measurements are approximate.) Refrigerate once again for 2–4 hours. Then make a strip 5 × 24 inches and cut out triangles with a pizza cutter to make about 12 croissants.

Roll the triangles into croissants very loosely with a big first fold in the base of the triangle. Give them room to expand and allow the peaks of the triangle to be up and out from under the croissant. Leaving the points up is best done by taking the two ends of the croissant with the tip of the fingers from each hand and twisting inward and up in midair as you set them on a pan.

The cooler the temperature the better it is to form these croissants. Keep them from warming up on the tray; put them in the oven fast with an egg glaze. The egg glaze gives them a shiny tan. With no egg glaze, they look pale and sickly.

Make the egg glaze by beating a whole egg or egg yolk with water. Paint the glaze on with a pastry brush or a new paint brush before you put the pastry in the oven to bake.

If you wish to use whole wheat flour in the croissant dough, it should not exceed 50 percent. Using whole wheat flour makes the croissants generally less flaky, sometimes even leatherlike. The success of these croissants is inconsistent and we find it a precarious endeavor. However, when filled with Cheese Herb Mix, Almond Cream, or Spinach Mix, they become edible and presentable.

Almond Croissant

Go back to the croissant recipe (page 90). When you reach the final strip of croissant dough which is 5 × 24 inches (page 94), spread the almond cream before you cut the triangle for the croissant. Roll the croissants loosely as they will be sticky. The almond cream will help lubricate the croissants so that they puff up as well as, if not better than, the plain croissants.

The more traditional recipe is to use old plain croissants. Slice them in 2 horizontally and dip the 2 halves in rum and maple syrup. Fill the middle of the split croissant with almond cream. Spread some almond cream over the top. Warm until the top almond cream has spread all over and warmth has penetrated the whole croissant. It is a lip-licker.

Almond Cream (Crème aux Amandes)

- *5 cups ground or sliced almonds*
- *1¼ lb. butter*
- *8 eggs*
- *3 cups granulated honey or sugar*
- *2 Tb. rum*
- *2 Tb. almond extract*

Cream butter with granulated honey or sugar. While whipping the buttercream, add all 8 eggs, the rum, and the almond extract. When smooth, mix in almonds and whip some more. If you have no ground almonds but sliced almonds instead, you may smash these sliced almonds as well as you can with a rolling pin, for example, and add this to the buttercream. This will result in a lacy almond crunch when it is cooked.

Almond cream can be used for croissant, almond twist (page 103), and to line the inside of a tart or pie crust underneath the fruit. A cooked pie shell with baked almond cream inside can then be filled with raw chopped fruit such as strawberries, raspberries, blueberries, etc., and then topped with a little whipped cream.

◆

☞ Note: Granulated or crystallized honey will cream with the butter successfully. Do not use liquid honey as it creams into butter very poorly.

96

Spinach Croissant

Spread the Spinach Mix with a spatula onto the 5 × 24 inch strip of ready croissant dough. Cut into triangles and bake as regular croissants.

◆

☞ Note that these croissants take longer than the others to cook.

Spinach Mix

This mix can be used for both turnovers and croissant.

- *1 lb. spinach (cooked and drained)*
- *12 oz. cottage cheese (or ricotta)*
- *1 Tb. chives (dried or fresh)*
- *1 Tb. parsley (dried or fresh)*
- *1 tsp. garlic powder*
- *1 tsp. Herb Mix*
- *2–3 oz. mozzarella or Parmesan*

Chop cooked spinach and mix in all other ingredients.

Cheese Herb Croissant

Again you have the strip of croissant dough 5 × 24 inches before you. Sprinkle on Cheese Herb Mix. Roll it into the dough with a slightly floured rolling pin. Then cut into triangles, egg-glaze, and cook the same as the plain croissant.

Cheese Herb Mix

This mix is for croissant or Puff Pastry Twists (page 102); it's also good for incorporating into the Spinach Mix above.

- *1 lb. Swiss cheese grated fine*
- *3 Tb. parsley flakes*
- *3 Tb. dried chives*
- *1 tsp. garlic powder*
- *2 tsp. Herb Mix (page 73) (optional)*

Hand mix all the above until mixture is unvarying in appearance and may be sprinkled. Note that all the herbs and garlic may be fresh chopped or minced for extra good flavor.

Goodness can flower only in
freedom. It cannot bloom in the
soil of persuasion in any form,
nor under compulsion, nor is it
the outcome of reward. It does
not reveal itself when there is any
kind of imitation or conformity,
and naturally it cannot exist when
there is fear.

Krishnamurti
from *Letters to the Schools*

Puff Pastry

Puff Pastry Dough (Pâte Feuilletée)

We find this pâte feuilletée the perfect substitute for phyllo dough.

The moisture content, although not as critical as in other recipes, must not exceed measurements indicated in the recipe. A firm dough is very rewarding and vital for warmer weather. If the temperature is hot (80°–90°F, 27°–32°C), it will be increasingly difficult to attain a good puff. As with all puffing (layering with butter), it is important to have all ingredients and environments as close as possible to 39°F (4°C).

- *3 lb. unbleached flour (11 cups)*
- *1 cup oil*
- *1 tsp. sea salt*
- *2½–3 cups water*
- *2–2½ lb. butter*

☞ Utensils:

- *large knife*
- *rolling pin*

Thoroughly blend in oil with the flour and salt. The oil makes the dough less elastic. We are trying, in this case, to have a less resilient dough. If you have flour which has the germ still in it, you will need less oil. However, all excess oil will separate with our procedure.

If you use any whole wheat flour, don't exceed 1 pound of whole wheat to 2 pounds of white flour until you feel you can manage with the excess whole wheat.

Mix blended flour and cool tap water as rapidly as possible. The electric mixer gives you the advantage of being able to trickle the water in as you mix. As soon as all the crumbs are picked up, stop pouring in the water. Set the dough in a container or plastic bag and put it in a cool place or refrigerator for overnight or several days. It will perform its best if you have the foresight to allow this dough to rest for several days.

When you get back to the dough, it may have a grayish yellow look and the oil may have separated from the surface. If the dough ferments at this point, it is best to discard the dough. Little gray specks in the dough do not mean fermentation. As soon as you roll the dough out, blemishes and specks will disappear. It should cooperate and spread out to a 16 × 32 inch rectangle with ease. Take 2 pounds of butter. (You may need an extra ½ pound of butter.) Slice the butter into slivers 2 × 2 inches by ⅛–¼ inch thick to cover ⅔ of the rectangle and lay the slivers on the dough. There is no need to cream or smash butter for this.

Fold the ⅓ without butter back over the buttered portion leaving ⅓ with butter still showing and fold that ⅓ over the rest. You will have at this point 2 layers of butter. You will have a piece of dough about 10 × 16 inches. Roll this out to 20 × 24 inches and fold in 3 giving a piece of dough 8 × 20 inches. Cut this in 2 and you will have 2 pieces of 8 × 10 inches. At this point you may freeze them for the future. When pulled out frozen, they must be thawed by resting overnight at 39°F (4°C). Avoid thawing out at room temperature for the puff will not puff well for you. It will become too soft and clammy and be heavy when cooked.

Let the dough rest a minimum of 2 hours at 39°F (4°C) or in the refrigerator overnight. Roll a piece out in 1 direction until it's about 3 times its width and fold this in 3. Then roll the length about 3 times *its* length and fold back in 3. At this point you should have a piece of dough that is once more 8 × 10 inches and ready to use after a 2 hour rest.

Freezing is okay before the last 2 foldings. Once folded for the last time and rested, you have many days to use it and the puff will be perfect. Freezing after these last 2 foldings is more complicated and we don't do it.

Cinnamon Twists

(makes approximately 20)

Take out a piece of Puff Pastry dough at its ready-to-use stage (page 101). Make sure to abundantly flour the surface you are working on. It is important to work fast especially in a warm environment. Roll out the piece of dough to 15 × 24 inches. Powder the cinnamon on the piece of dough, then sprinkle on sugar and spread them out evenly with your hand. Roll it with the rolling pin to assure that the cinnamon and sugar remains on the puff dough when folding. Fold on the wide side (15-inch side) creating a piece of dough 7½ × 24 inches. Roll out the width a couple more inches thus having a 9 × 24 inch rectangle.

Cut 1¼ × 9 inch strips with a pizza cutter along the width. Give them a gentle twist in midair and place on an oiled or lined sheet pan. These may be baked at temperatures between 350° and 450°F (175°–232°C). For the hotter temperatures, you must watch them attentively. When they get stiff and dry in appearance, they are done. Other fillings may be used such as the Cheese Herb Mix (page 97) or the Almond Cream (page 96).

Cheese Herb Twists

(makes approximately 20)

As with the piece of puff described in Cinnamon Twists, sprinkle the Cheese Herb Mixture evenly. Roll it in with a slightly floured rolling pin. Do exactly as with the Cinnamon Twist.

This twist will be done when the bits of cheese turn golden but not brown.

Almond Cream Twists
(makes approximately 20)

The almond cream needs to be at room temperature (68°F, 20°C). Roll the Puff Pastry dough out to make a 15 × 24 inch rectangle. Spread the almond cream generously with a spatula on half the dough, covering a portion that measures 7½ × 24 inches. Fold the plain half over the creamed half. Roll this gently with a rolling pin to even out the wrinkles. The result is a smooth 7½ × 24 inch slab of dough with almond cream in the middle.

Spread a thin layer of almond cream on top of the piece of dough; this will make the surface tacky. Spread sliced almonds on top of the tacky surface and gently press them down with a rolling pin. Cut out 1¼ × 7½ inch strips with a pizza cutter preferably. Give them a half-turn twist at each end before placing them on an oiled sheet pan. Bake at 350–450°F (175°–232°C) until the almond cream turns brown (15–20 minutes).

More or less sad are finally all
those who are aware of things
beyond questions of daily bread;
but who would wish to live without
this sadness, deep and still,
without which there is no true joy.

Springs of Joy
by Gottfried Keller

The Quick Blender Breads

Three Quick Breads

The following three recipes were inspired by Bob Brewer of Ontario, Canada. The procedure for the following 3 breads is identical.

◆

Preheat oven to 400°F (205°C) and make sure your oven rack is placed in the middle. Place bread in oven and reduce heat to 350°F (175°C) for metal pan and 325°F (160°C) for glass pan.

Oil the pan and set aside.

Measure dry ingredients in a large bowl. Scoop unsifted flour lightly into a measuring cup and level off with a spatula. Do not level off flour by shaking the cup. It will pack the flour and increase the quantity, and the result will be a heavier drier bread.

Combine the wet ingredients in a blender. Then add all at once to the dry ingredients and hand mix gently until the flour is incorporated.

Bake by placing pan on a middle oven rack that does not touch the side of the oven. Test with toothpick to ensure they are done. Remove and let cool 10 minutes. Then remove from pan and let cool on wire rack.

Applesauce Bread

☞ Mix in a large bowl:

- *2 cups flour (whole wheat)*
- *¾ cup maple syrup (or sugar)*
- *1 Tb. baking powder (double acting)*
- *1 tsp. sea salt*
- *½ tsp. cinnamon*
- *½ tsp. baking soda*

☞ Place the following in blender:

- *1 egg*
- *1 Tb. oil or butter*
- *2–3 chopped apples, including skin, seeds, and core (no stems)*

Blend and add cider to make 20 fluid ounces. Add wet mixture to dry mixture and hand mix. Bake at 350°F (175°C) for 1 hour. Test at the 45 minute mark.

Carrot Bread

☞ Mix in a large bowl:

- *1½ cups flour (whole wheat)*
- *1 tsp. baking powder (double acting)*
- *1 tsp. baking soda*
- *1 tsp. cinnamon*
- *1 cup maple syrup (or sugar)*

☞ Shred carrots in a food processor. Then fit with mixer blade and combine the remaining wet ingredients:

- *1–2 cups shredded carrots*
- *2 eggs*
- *½ cup salad oil*
- *½ cup cider*

Add wet mixture to dry mixture and hand mix. Bake at 350°F (175°C) for 50 minutes or until done.

Banana Bread

☞ Mix in a large bowl:

- *2 cups flour (whole wheat)*
- *¾ cup maple syrup*
- *1 tsp. sea salt*
- *1 tsp. baking soda*
- *1 tsp. baking powder*

☞ Place the following in blender:

- *3 ripe bananas*
- *2 eggs*
- *2 Tb. oil or butter*

Blend and add an ounce of orange juice if it needs help blending.

Add wet mixture to dry mixture and hand mix. Oil pan and bake 1 hour at 350°F (175°C). Test at the 45 minute mark.

There will be further changes
when the computer is fully
developed. You are just at the
beginning of it. Then when
the computer takes over what
is going to happen to our
human minds?

Krishnamurti

Potpourri

Chocolate Chip Cookies

(makes 24 large cookies)

- ¾ lb. butter
- 1 cup packed brown sugar
- 1 egg
- 1 cup chocolate chips (or carob, butterscotch or vanilla chips)
- ½ cup sunflower seeds
- ½ cup sesame seeds
- ½ cup walnut pieces
- 2 tsp. molasses
- ¼ cup juice (orange, pineapple) or milk (optional)
- 2 ½ cups flour
- 1 tsp. baking powder
- an ice cream or cookie scoop with a 3-tablespoon capacity

Cool ingredients make a good cookie. Cream the butter with the brown sugar. Add the egg immediately followed by the chips, seeds, nuts, molasses, and juice until well mixed. Stir in the flour with the baking powder and a pinch of salt.

Scoop the dough with a 3-tablespoon ice cream scoop and place on a lined or lightly greased pan 4–5 inches apart. Dip your three fingers in a glass of cool water and squash the batter flat on the sheet pan to make a flattened ball about 2½ inches in diameter.

Bake for about 20 minutes in an oven at 350°F (175°C). The finished cookie will be 3½–4 inches in diameter.

If cooked on the lighter side, until the very edges get light brown, the cookies will be very chewy for the remainder of that day. These cookies, however, are more of a short cookie and keep for a month in a tin under cool and dry conditions. If you make this batch of cookies without the egg, you will have a rich crunchy cookie.

Lenten Cookies

- *1 cup oil*
- *1 cup maple syrup or fruit juice concentrate (fructose) or honey*
- *2 cups whole wheat flour*
- *2 cups oatmeal*
- *1 tsp. baking powder*
- *1 tsp. baking soda*
- *1 tsp. cinnamon*
- *½ tsp. nutmeg*
- *1 cup walnuts*
- *2 cups raisins*

These cookies are for those who do not want to eat any animal products (honey included). Honey works the best for those who want it.

Simply blend all the above ingredients until it sticks together in a puttylike fashion. A small mixer will do the trick without effort. Place small balls of the dough on an oiled sheet pan and flatten with wet fingers. This recipe makes 30 or more cookies. Cook them well at 350°F (175°C) for 10–20 minutes. Allow them to cool before moving them about. They have a meringue like look and are quite brittle.

Whole Wheat Oatmeal Cookies

(makes 24 large cookies)

☞ Keep ingredients cool.

- *½ lb. butter (using oil instead of butter will make a crumbly cookie)*
- *½ cup honey (granulated if possible)*
- *½ cup maple syrup*
- *2 eggs*
- *2 cups whole wheat flour*
- *2 cups oatmeal*
- *1 tsp. baking soda*
- *1 tsp. baking powder*
- *1 tsp. cinnamon*
- *½ tsp. nutmeg*
- *½ cup walnuts*
- *1 cup raisins*

Blend butter with honey and maple syrup. Add eggs to the butter cream. Add all the dry ingredients and stir thoroughly. (Using cool ingredients will give better results. Crystallized honey will cream better and give a more crispy cookie.)

With a small ice cream scoop, place balls on a greased or lined tray and flatten them down with wet fingers. Bake at 350°F (175°C) for about 10–15 minutes. They should brown up a little.

Granola

- *5 cups oatmeal (rolled oats)*
- *1 cup wheat germ*
- *1 cup wheat flakes*
- *¼ cup soy flakes or soy flour*
- *1 cup sunflower seeds*
- *½ cup sliced almonds*
- *⅓ cup pepitas (pumpkin seeds)*
- *⅓ cup sesame seeds*
- *1 cup soy oil*
- *½ cup maple syrup vanilla extract or ground vanilla can go in the syrup*

Mix all the dry ingredients with mixer or by hand. Add the oil, mix thoroughly, then add the syrup. Mix the granola until the grains begin to cling together. If it looks too dry for your taste, add more oil or syrup or both. Always mix the oil in before the syrup.

The advantage of having an electric mixer, especially for larger quantities, is that it evenly breaks up and distributes the ingredients. Mix for a maximum of 5 minutes. You will have meal instead of granola if it goes longer.

Put granola mixture, unpacked, ½–¾ of an inch deep into a flat pan. Note that the granola in the corners of the pans will burn before the middle is cooked. To avoid burning the corners and/or having to stir the mixture, do not put granola into the corners of the pans. Then bake 30 minutes at 300°–350°F (150°–175°C) or when golden brown with a lot of crumbly chunks. The granola doesn't have to be evenly roasted. Cool the granola before storing. The oil will turn rancid if stored while hot.

This recipe can be made by substituting another sweetener for the maple syrup. Other sweeteners must be made into syrup form before adding to the granola.

Old Cavendish Fruitcake

- ½ lb. butter
- 1⅛ lb. honey
- 5 eggs

- 2 cups flour
- 1 tsp. baking powder
- ½ tsp. salt
- 1 tsp. cinnamon
- ½ tsp. allspice

- ½ lb. walnuts
- ½ lb. cashews
- ¾ lb. unsulphured apricots
- ⅔ lb. raisins
- ½ lb. prunes
- ½ lb. dates

- ½ cup orange juice
- ¼ cup light cream
- 1 Tb. lemon juice

- ½ cup brandy
- ½ cup orange liqueur

Have eggs, butter, and honey at room temperature. Preheat oven to 275°F (135°C). Chop fruit into small pieces. Cream butter and honey until light and frothy. Add eggs and beat until light.

In a separate bowl, sift dry ingredients and add ½ to butter and honey mix. Add fruits and nuts to remaining flour.

Combine light cream with lemon and orange juice and add to butter and honey mix. Fold in remaining fruit and nuts to butter and honey mix.

Pour into tube or springform pans. Bake at 275°F (135°C) for 2½–3 hours (three 2-pound loaves). When the cakes are cool sprinkle ⅓ cup of combined brandy and liqueur on each cake.

Remove cakes from pans after brandy and liqueur mix has soaked in. Wrap in plastic and chill for 6 weeks.

Boston Brown Bread

- 4 cups Rye Mix (page 40)
- 4 cups cornmeal (whole)
- 4 cups whole wheat flour
- 2 tsp. baking soda
- 3 cups molasses (use only unsulphured molasses)
- 2 Tb. sea salt
- 8 cups buttermilk or 8 cups milk with ½ cup vinegar
- 1 cup raisins (optional)

You will need your neighbor's canner or a clam steamer for this recipe.

Place the brown bread batter in pans or tins, covered with foil or a lid, into already boiling water or in with the baking beans. Patience is required for the cooking. Depending on the sizes and shapes of the tins, it will take 30 minutes to 1 hour or until the topmost centers of the breads are done.

Crêpe Soyette

- *2 cups whole wheat flour*
- *2 cups soy milk*
- *2 eggs*
- *1 Tb. tamari (soy sauce)*
- *2 Tb. apple cider (especially hard cider; any beer can replace the apple cider and even some of the soy milk)*
- *4 Tb. orange juice*
- *2 Tb. soy oil or blend*
- *½ cup soy flour*
- *1 Tb. honey or maple syrup*

It is preferable to put the sweetener on top of the cooked crêpe, because sugars incorporated in the batter will brown and cause the crêpes to burn and stick more easily.

Stir the 2 eggs into the whole wheat, making a paste. As the batter gets thicker, add tamari, orange juice, and a ½ cup of the soy milk to keep it free of lumps. Once all the flour is incorporated into the batter, add the remaining liquid to make a runny consistency.

The ratio of 1 egg to 1 cup of flour to 1 cup of soy milk makes batter for any kind of crêpe. The recipe can be made without the eggs; the crêpes then tend to break much more easily and require more care in flipping and handling.

☞ Utensils:
- *any iron skillet*
- *hot mittens*
- *a bowl*
- *a ½ cup measure*
- *a spoon or whisk*
- *a spatula*

This recipe makes approximately 1 quart. One-half cup will make a 10-inch crêpe. The whole recipe makes 7 full crêpes plus a little one. The little crêpe is to test the temperature of the frying pan. This first little one traditionally goes to the dog (au chien). Get the skillet very hot with a dab of oil. Pour the batter into the middle of the frying pan. Slowly twirl the pan so that the batter sweeps the whole bottom inside of the pan. Flip them over when a lacy, brown pattern has developed on their undersides. When cooked, stack them on a plate to cool and then roll them up with fruits, etc.

◆

☞ Suggestion: To one sauteed onion, add 2 cups of sliced mushrooms, 1 tablespoon of whole wheat flour, and a pinch of cayenne pepper. Once this mixture is cooked, spread on a crêpe and roll up.

Tofu Paté

- *1 lb. firm tofu*
- *¼ lb. soft butter*
- *2 lightly beaten eggs*
- *1 Tb. tamari (soy sauce)*
- *2 Tb. oil to saute*
- *1 medium onion*
- *½ tsp. thyme*
- *1 tsp. chives*
- *1 tsp. parsley*
- *1 pinch allspice*
- *1 tsp. mixed herbs*
- *⅛ tsp. pepper*
- *½ cup cognac*

Saute onion in the 2 tablespoons of oil. In a blender, put all the spices, the ½ cup of cognac, the tamari, and the sauteed onion. Then add the eggs and continue blending while adding alternate portions of tofu and butter. It will form a thick paste. Scrape into a paté mold, cheesecake mold, or a pyrex dish with or without puff pastry lining. Cook in oven at moderate heat (350°F, 175°C) for 60 minutes. Excess butter will flow out of the molds so take care to put a pan underneath.

◆

☞ Optional: Before cooking, submerge hard boiled eggs, pitted olives, sauteed mushrooms, etc. into the paté.

In the Egypt of 2300 BC to
give bread was such a noble,
good, and saintly thing to do that
they used the symbol for bread
(pictograph or hieroglyphics)
in the expression "to give."

Musée du Pain

Hall of Receipts

The Hall of Receipts is for camps, schools, and restaurants who use mixers of 30- to 60-quart capacity or more. The following recipes are exactly the ones we use at the Baba À Louis Bakeries with our 60-quart mixers. At Baba À Louis Bakery, the soured yeast breads are mixed at 4 PM and are put in covered tubs to rise until 3 AM the next morning. The unsoured yeast breads are mixed at 6 AM to be finished that same morning. The unsoured yeast breads are baked along with the soured ones so that the entire baking process will be finished by noon.

The bread ingredients must be weighed on an accurate scale. A container which holds 12 quarts is needed for weighing the dry ingredients and a tub which holds 12 gallons (per batch) is needed for the rising. All the weights of the dry ingredients will be given without including the container's weight.

◆

☞ Note that the flour used for the following recipes is bakers' bread flour. (See About Flour, page 30.)

Previous page: Ancient Egyptian bread making depicted on King Ramses II tomb (funerary painting). The repetition and sequences of the pictographs in this scene would imply a recipe on a large scale.

Basic French Bread

(makes seventeen 1½-pound loaves)

- *19½ lb. unbleached white flour*
- *¾ cup sea salt*
- *2 Tb. instant yeast (page 24) (2½ Tb. dry yeast)*
- *20 cups water, anywhere from body temperature to 120°F (48°C), (19 cups cold water in summer heat)*

Refer to page 29 for Basic French Bread recipe. Allow 12 hours for the dough to rise.

Lenten Bread

(makes 8 loaves in pans only)

- *3½ lb. Rye Mix (page 40)*
- *2 lb. whole wheat flour*
- *9 cups water, anywhere from body temperature to 120°F (48°C)*
- *2 Tb. ground or pulped wakame sea weed or others*
- *2 Tb. caraway seeds*

Allow to sit for 12 hours (note no yeast). Mix in 3 pounds of Basic French Bread dough which has also risen 12 hours. After a small rising time put in loaf pans.

Carababa

(makes 12 loaves)

- *10 lb. unbleached white flour*
- *1 lb. whole wheat mix*
- *1 lb. Rye Mix (page 40)*
- *1 cup caraway seeds*
- *½ cup sea salt*
- *1 Tb. instant yeast (page 24) (1½ Tb. dry yeast)*
- *12 cups water, anywhere from body temperature to 120°F (48°C)*

Allow 12 hours for the dough to rise. (See small recipe for further instructions, page 48.)

Sticky Bun Dough

(makes 10–11 bags of 4 pounds each)

- *26 lb. unbleached white flour*
- *3 lb. butter or margarine (melted)*
- *40 eggs*
- *2 Tb. instant yeast (page 24) (2½ Tb. dry yeast)*
- *6 cups sugar or maple syrup*
- *2 Tb. sea salt*
- *20 cups water, anywhere from body temperature to 120°F (48°C)*

Place in oiled plastic bags to freeze or to rise. (See instructions for small recipe, page 79.)

Anadama Bread

(makes about 16 loaves)

- *15 lb. unbleached white flour*
- *2 Tb. instant yeast (page 24) (2½ Tb. dry yeast)*
- *2 Tb. sea salt*
- *1 cup soy flour*
- *2 cups wheat bran*
- *1 cup oil*
- *4½ cups whole cornmeal (with germ)*
- *16 cups water, anywhere from body temperature to 120°F (48°C)*
- *2 cups blackstrap molasses*

Poppy Louis

(makes 12 loaves)

- *10 lb. unbleached white flour*
- *1 lb. whole wheat mix*
- *1 lb. Rye Mix (page 40)*
- *1 cup poppy seeds*
- *12 cups water, anywhere from body temperature to 120°F (48°C) (use cold water in summer heat)*
- *½ cup sea salt*
- *1 Tb. instant yeast (page 24) (1½ Tb. dry yeast)*

Allow 12 hours for the dough to rise. (See small recipe for further instructions, page 44.)

Maur's Rye

(makes 13–14 loaves)

- *4 lb. Rye Mix*
- *3½ lb. whole wheat (Whitmer* if possible)*
- *3 lb. unbleached white flour*
- *2 Tb. sea salt*
- *2 Tb. caraway seeds*
- *2 Tb. seaweed (powdered or shredded)*
- *¾ Tb. instant yeast (page 24) (1 Tb. dry yeast)*
- *14 cups water, anywhere from body temperature to 120°F (48°C) (use cold water in summer heat)*

Three pounds of Basic French Bread dough (page 35), just mixed, kneaded in that same night. Allow 12 hours for the dough to rise.

*Whitmer whole wheat flour takes more water than other whole wheat flours.

Six Grain and One Bean
(makes about 17 loaves)

☞ Soak overnight in 5 cups water:

- *3 cups oatmeal*
- *1½ cups cracked wheat*
- *1½ cups Rye Mix (page 40)*
- *1½ cups soy flour*
- *1½ cups barley*
- *1½ cups bulgar wheat*
- *1½ cups millet*
- *1½ cups cornmeal*
- *4 cups sprouted wheat (½-inch sprouts) (alfalfa sprouts may be used)*

☞ Next morning mix with:

- *15 lb. whole wheat*
- *1 cup oil*
- *2 Tb. sea salt*
- *2 Tb. instant yeast (page 24) (2½ Tb. dry yeast)*
- *15 cups water, anywhere from body temperature to 120°F (48°C)*

(See small recipe for further instructions, page 76.)

Raisin Bread
(makes about 16 loaves)

- *15 lb. unbleached white flour*
- *2 Tb. instant yeast (page 24) (2½ Tb. dry yeast)*
- *2 Tb. sea salt*
- *2 cups oil*
- *2 cups wheat bran*
- *1 cup soy flour*
- *4 cups raisins (at least)*
- *16 cups water, anywhere from body temperature to 120°F (48°C)*

For rolling bread you will need melted butter, cinnamon, and brown sugar. (See small recipe for further instructions, page 75.)

Oatmeal

(makes about 19 loaves)

- *15 lb. unbleached white flour*
- *1 cup soy flour*
- *1 cup oil (soy)*
- *2 cups bran (wheat)*
- *2 Tb. sea salt*
- *2 Tb. instant yeast (page 24) (2½ Tb. dry yeast)*
- *22 cups water, anywhere from body temperature to 120°F (48°C)*

When well mixed, add 16 cups oatmeal until well dispersed. (See small recipe for further instructions, page 70.)

Cheese Herb Bread

(makes about 16 loaves)

White bread may be made from this recipe by omitting the chives, parsley, garlic powder, Herb Mix, and cheese.

- *15 lb. unbleached white flour*
- *2 Tb. instant yeast (page 24) (2½ Tb. dry yeast)*
- *2 Tb. sea salt*
- *1 cup soy flour*
- *2 cups wheat bran*
- *2 cups oil*
- *4 Tb. dry or fresh chives*
- *4 Tb. dry or fresh parsley*
- *2 Tb. garlic powder*
- *2 Tb. Herb Mix (page 73)*
- *12–16 oz. cheese (mozzarella or as indicated in the small version of recipe on page 73)*
- *17–18 cups water, anywhere from body temperature to 120°F (48°C)*

(See small recipe for further instructions, page 73.)

Loaf Rye

(makes about 16 loaves)

- 6 lb. Rye Mix (page 40)
- 9 lb. unbleached white flour
- 2 Tb. sea salt
- 2 Tb. instant yeast (page 24) (2½ Tb. dry yeast)
- 1 cup soy flour
- 2 cups wheat bran
- 2 cups oil (soy)
- 2 cups molasses (blackstrap)
- 2 cups honey
- 8 Tb. caraway seeds
- 18 cups water, anywhere from body temperature to 120°F (48°C)

Very sticky dough. (See small recipe for further instructions, page 81.)

Swedish Rye (Limpa)

(makes about 10 loaves)

- 8 lb. unbleached white flour
- 3 lb. Rye Mix (page 40)
- 2 Tb. instant yeast (page 24) (2½ Tb. dry yeast)
- 1 Tb. cardamom powder
- 2 Tb. sea salt
- 1 cup orange juice
- 1 cup oil
- 1½–2 cups molasses
- 8 cups water, anywhere from body temperature to 120°F (48°C)

Brush the tops with butter. (See small recipe for further instructions, page 77.)

Sour Wheat Barley (Whole Wheat French)

(makes twenty-five 1½-pound loaves)

- *10½ lb. whole wheat flour (Whitmer) with some cracked wheat (optional)*
- *9 lb. unbleached white flour*
- *3 cups barley soaked and soured or just precooked*
- *⅔ cup sea salt*
- *2 Tb. instant yeast (page 24) (2½ Tb. dry yeast)*
- *19 cups water, anywhere from body temperature to 120°F (48°C) (use cold water in summer heat)*
- *15 lb. Basic French Bread dough (page 121).*

Knead the Basic French dough with mixture above until completely mixed. Note that the Basic French dough may just have been mixed. Allow 12 hours for the dough to rise. (See small recipe for further instructions, page 44.)

Open Sesame Bread (à la Baba)

Combine excess Sour Wheat Barley dough (page 128) with Basic French Bread dough (page 121), which have both had a 12-hour rise. To a ratio of 3 parts Sour Wheat Barley dough to 1 part Basic French Bread dough, mix in 1 pound of roasted sesame seeds (hulled or unhulled) for every 8–12 loaves (1½ pounds of dough to each loaf of bread). (See small recipe for further instructions, page 49.)

Walnut Bread

Use the Sour Wheat Barley (page 128) which has been allowed 12 hours to rise and add 1 pound (4 cups) of walnut halves and pieces to every 4 loaves of bread (6 pounds of dough).

If a ratio of 1 pound of Basic French Bread dough (page 121) to 2–3 pounds of Sour Wheat Barley (Whole Wheat French) is used and the mixing is stopped before the dough becomes homogeneous, a beautiful marble effect will occur which improves the presentation and texture of the bread. (See small recipe for further instructions, page 52 .)

Spinach Turnover and Croissant Mix

- *6 lb. spinach (cooked and drained)*
- *5 lb. cottage cheese*
- *12–16 oz. grated mozzarella*
- *4 Tb. chives*
- *4 Tb. parsley*
- *1 Tb. garlic powder*
- *1 Tb. Herb Mix (page 73)*

Chop cooked spinach and mix in all other ingredients. Use an ice cream scoop for turnover or wooden spoon to spread for croissant.

Pumpernickel

(makes 8 round loaves of 1½ pound each and will fit on a standard sheet pan)

- 13 lb. Sourdough Rye (just made)
- 1 lb. coarse rye steeped in ¾ cup warm water for 1 hour or so
- 2 Tb. cocoa
- ¾ cup blackstrap molasses

Knead all together and set in tub for the 12-hour rise. (See small recipe for further instructions, page 46.)

Sourdough Rye

(makes twenty-five 1½-pound loaves)

- 6½ lb. Rye Mix (page 40)
- 13 lb. unbleached white flour
- ¾ cup sea salt
- 2 Tb. instant yeast (page 24) (2½ Tb. dry yeast)
- 4 Tb. caraway seeds
- 20 cups water, anywhere from body temperature to 120°F (48°C) (19 cups cold water in summer heat)
- 15 lb. Basic French Bread dough (page 121) just mixed and kneaded in that same night. Allow 12 hours for the dough to rise.

(See small recipe for further instructions, page 42.)

Oat Bran Bread

(makes about 19 loaves)

- 15 lb. unbleached white flour
- 1 cup soy flour
- 1 cup soy oil
- 2 cups wheat bran
- 2 Tb. sea salt
- 2 Tb. instant yeast (page 24) (2½ Tb. dry yeast)
- 10 cups oatmeal
- 8 cups oat bran
- ¼ cup molasses (optional)
- 21 cups water, anywhere from body temperature to 120°F (48°C)

Reserve 5 cups of oatmeal and add after the other ingredients have been well mixed. It is better to have more oats than oat bran. (See small recipe for further instructions, page 71.)

Fruit Fiber Bread

(makes 18 loaves)

☞ Wet Mixture:

- *4 cups frozen cranberries or soaked fresh cranberries (blueberries make a good substitute)*
- *2 cups walnut pieces*
- *6 cup chopped dates*
- *½ cup honey*
- *6 cups water to soak one hour or overnight*
- *15 lb. unbleached white flour*
- *4 cups oat bran*
- *4 cups oatmeal*
- *1 cup honey*
- *2 Tb. sea salt*
- *2 Tb. instant yeast (page 24) (2½ Tb. dry yeast)*
- *1 cup soy flour*
- *2 cups wheat bran*
- *1 cup oil*
- *15–16 cups water, anywhere from body temperature to 120°F (48°C)*

Reserve ½ cup of cranberries in a separate container to add at the end of the kneading to assure whole pieces of cranberries in the mixed bread. (See small recipe for further instructions, page 80.)

Peter's Grain Bread

(makes 20 loaves)

Cook 2 cups of millet. Drain the cooked millet and allow it to cool. Soak the following ingredients for ½ hour:

- *8 cups oatmeal*
- *4 cups bulgur wheat*
- *6 cups wheat flakes*
- *4 cups sunflower seeds*
- *2 cups molasses*
- *8 cups water*

Use 22½ lb. of newly made Sour Wheat Barley dough. Knead together the dough, the soaked grain and the cooked millet until it is all an even color.

Allow 12 hours for the dough to rise. (See small recipe for further instructions, page 53.)

Book development, design, and production:
The Laughing Bear Associates, Montpelier, Vermont

Editing Services:
Olivia Gay
Kate Mueller

Formatting:
Electric Dragon Productions, Montpelier, Vermont

Printing:
Northlight Studio Press, Barre, Vermont

Book distribution:
Chelsea Green Publishing Company, Post Mills, Vermont

Photography:
Allesandro Zezza and Tonya Sammartino, 21, 33, 34, 35,
    36 (top, left), 37 (right), 38, 39, 40, 43, 48, 50, 51, 55,
    61, 69, 78, 89, 99, 105, 109, 115, 121, 122, 129
Mary McCallum, 23, 36 (right, top and bottom), 37 (left)
John McLure, front cover, 66, 83
Ellen Foscue Johnson, 27 (courtesy of the photographer, from
    Garden Way Bread Book)

Original illustrations:
Ed Epstein, 90–95

Historical illustrations and photographs:
Roger-Viollet, 12, 14, 19